EAST AND WEST IN RELIGION

by RADHAKRISHNAN

INDIAN PHILOSOPHY
THE HINDU VIEW OF LIFE
AN IDEALIST VIEW OF LIFE
THE RECOVERY OF FAITH
THE BRAHMA SUTRA
THE CONCEPT OF MAN
EAST AND WEST IN RELIGION
RELIGION AND SOCIETY
THE BHAGAVADGĪTĀ
EAST AND WEST: SOME REFLECTIONS
(Allen and Unwin)
EASTERN RELIGIONS AND WESTERN THOUGHT
(Clarendon Press, Oxford)
THE DHAMMAPADA
(Oxford University Press)
INDIA AND CHINA
IS THIS PEACE?
GREAT INDIANS
(Hind Kitabs, Bombay)
THE PRINCIPAL UPANIṢADS

edited by RADHAKRISHNAN

MAHATMA GANDHI
(Allen and Unwin)
HISTORY OF PHILOSOPHY EASTERN AND WESTERN
2 Vols.
(Allen and Unwin)

edited by RADHAKRISHNAN and J. H. MUIRHEAD

CONTEMPORARY INDIAN PHILOSOPHY
(Allen and Unwin)

by A. N. MARLOW

RADHAKRISHNAN: AN ANTHOLOGY

S. RADHAKRISHNAN

EAST AND WEST
IN
RELIGION

GEORGE ALLEN & UNWIN LTD
RUSKIN HOUSE · MUSEUM STREET · LONDON

FIRST PUBLISHED IN 1933
SECOND IMPRESSION IN 1949
THIRD IMPRESSION IN 1954
FOURTH IMPRESSION IN 1958
FIFTH IMPRESSION IN 1967

PRINTED IN GREAT BRITAIN
BY JOHN DICKENS AND CO LTD
NORTHAMPTON

TO MY FRIEND
L. P. JACKS

AUTHOR'S NOTE

Dr. J. H. Muirhead and Dr. J. E. Turner very kindly read the proofs of this book and I am greatly indebted to them.

S. R.

CONTENTS

LECTURE I

COMPARATIVE RELIGION

LECTURE I

COMPARATIVE RELIGION[1]

I AM greatly indebted to the authorities of Manchester College and Oxford University for granting me this opportunity to deliver a course of lectures on the philosophy of religion treated from the comparative point of view. It is specially appropriate that this subject should be studied in this great seat of learning where its foundations were laid in the later part of the nineteenth century.

I

THE GROWTH OF THE SCIENCE

The development of the science of Comparative Religion is due mainly to two factors:—the publication and study of the Sacred Books of the East, and the growth of anthropology. Both owe their inspiration to great Oxford teachers. That intrepid investigator of Indo-Aryan religions, Frederick Max Müller, gave an impetus to the study of Comparative Religion by his own lectures on the subject as well as by the publication of the fifty volumes of the Sacred Books of the East. Max Müller describes these

[1] This lecture is the first of a series on Comparative Religion given at Manchester College, Oxford, on October 22, 1929.

lectures on the Science of Religion as "an introduction to the comparative study of the principal
religions of the world."[1] His great work was
continued by the patient and scholarly investigations
of Dr. Estlin Carpenter of this college, especially
with reference to Indian Theism and the relations
between Buddhism and Christianity; and so long as
we continue to cultivate this branch of study,
Carpenter's name will be remembered with genuine
gratitude.

By his works on *Primitive Culture* and *Anthropology*
the other great Oxford Professor, Sir Edward Tylor,
opened out the anthropological approach to the
study of religion. Sir James Frazer's monumental
works on *The Golden Bough, Totemism and Exogamy*
bring together a mass of material invaluable for the
study of religious origins and growth. It is unnecessary for me to refer to the writings of the many
anthropologists whose studies of the beliefs and
customs of savages and primitive tribes throw a
flood of light on man's early attempts to discern the
hidden purpose of the universe. It is a pleasure to
note that the study of anthropology inaugurated in
this University by Sir Edward Tylor is so ably
represented to-day by Dr. Marett.

The doctrine of evolution stimulated the growth
of the science of anthropology and so, indirectly, of
Comparative Religion. Anthropology discovers that

[1] *Introduction to the Science of Religion* (New Impression, 1909),
p. 7.

14

the general movement is one of progress from crude and less complex stages to more refined and developed forms. For it religion is a phase of human culture obeying the same laws as do other social institutions.[1] Among other factors which are responsible for the progress of the study of Comparative Religion may be mentioned the decipherment of the Assyrian, Babylonian and Egyptian texts. The work of foreign Christian missions, similarly, is not inconsiderable. They have furnished us with careful and competent accounts of the religious beliefs and practices of lower tribes and primitive communities.

II

ALLEGED OBJECTIONS TO THE STUDY

But when we speak of Comparative Religion we do not mean that it is a special kind of religion; it is only a particular method of treating religion. The comparative method itself has been adopted with conspicuous success in such varied departments of knowledge as anatomy and psychology, philology and jurisprudence, and recently we have had a book by a French writer on comparative Philosophy.[2] And yet protests are heard now and again against a comparative study of religion.

One reason for this is that the scientific study of

[1] See Marett: *Anthropology* (1912), chap. i.
[2] Professor M. P. Masson-Oursel.

religion is imagined to be a danger to religion itself.
For a scientific student of religion is required to treat
all religions in a spirit of absolute detachment and
impartiality. To him one religion is as good as
another; but such an attitude of cold neutrality in
matters of religion does not appeal to the majority
of mankind. Religion, it is argued, is nothing if not
partisan and particularist. To compare the sacred
books of the East with the holy scriptures of the
West is to ignore that feeling of warmth and reverence which each individual has for his own religion.
To such an objection it must be replied that truth
is higher than any religion and a truly scientific
attitude in these matters will ultimately result in
gain immeasurably greater than any loss we may
incur in the process. At the same time, while we
may surrender our exclusive claims, the religion in
which we were brought up will still exert a peculiar
charm and fascination over us.

Another objection is that comparison means
resemblance; and if one religion is like another,
what happens to the claims of superiority and
uniqueness? Certainly Comparative Religion notes
the facts of resemblance as well as of difference. But
a recognition of the points of similarity does not
mean that the points of difference are negligible.
Even if we wish to set forth the superior claims of
one religion, it is necessary for us to know and
appreciate the claims and contents of others.

Again, it is urged, if Comparative Religion tells

16

us that higher religions possess features in common with the low and the primitive, then the inference is legitimate that our religious beliefs are of a degrading and childish character. For example, Constantine's conversion to Christianity, which led to its triumph, was not quite assured for some considerable time. He hesitated a good deal between Mithra and Jesus, because the two religions of Mithraism and Christianity very closely resembled each other. Like Jesus, Mithra was a mediator between God and men whose salvation was assured by a sacrifice. The Mithraists believed in a moral law and a future life as firmly as Christians. Tertullian, who attributed the close resemblance of the two to the artifices of the devil, was specially scandalized by the Mithraic rite of the consecration of bread and wine. Further, many primitive religions believed in the sacrificial death of the god, and the communion meal of the faithful with the divine body was literal and actual whenever the god of the tribes was an animal. By eating an animal, a hero or a god, devotees were believed to acquire their appropriate qualities. Thus the rites of sacrifice and communion which are the very bases of Christianity can be traced to such primitive beliefs. Here again all that need be said is that it is illogical to confuse questions of origin and of value. The tracing of the historical derivation of religious ideas is quite different from a critical determination of their value. Besides, even in the most backward races there are deep stirrings and dim yearnings after God which may be cruelly distorted, but nevertheless are there. We may derive spiritual illumination even from dark places. Comparative Religion postulates that all our faiths have some value. It is unnecessary for me to urge this upon you, at any rate not in this college which stands for a policy of free discussion in religion.

In the end, therefore, those who are disturbed by the results of the study of Comparative Religion will thank it for its labours. For it proves beyond doubt that while there are innumerable changes in religious forms, religion itself is found to be a universal phenomenon. Right round the world, distributed more or less uniformly, we find a mass of faith and ritual which, in spite of apparent variations and individual forms, seem to cohere with respect to certain essential features. Religion is native to the human mind, integral to human nature itself. Everything else may dissolve; but belief in God, which is the ultimate confession of all the faiths of the world, remains. Though religion may take many forms, it will continue as long as man remains what he is, a blend of power and weakness. The earliest manifestations of religion revealed in the study of anthropology confirm this. The general consent of mankind, the universal longing of human souls which has been used as a proof of the existence of God, receives impressive ratification by the results of Comparative Religion. When the Athenian stranger asked the Cretan Cleinias in Plato's *Laws* to prove the existence of the gods, the latter put forward two arguments:—(i) the fair order of the universe and the regularity of the seasons, and (ii) the common belief of all men, Hellenes and Barbarians. Behind all the varied expressions, Brahman, Yahveh, Ahuramazda, Allah, there is the same intention, the same striving, the same faith. All religions spring from the sacred soil of the human mind and are quickened by the same spirit. The different systems are tentative adjustments, more or less satisfactory, to spiritual reality. Comparative Religion accounts for their similarities by affirming that the human spirit feels after the same spiritual reality, and is in some manner acted upon by it. Thus, while Comparative Religion may not support orthodoxy, it does not shelter unbelief.

III

VALUE OF THE STUDY

Comparative Religion tells us that all religions have had a history and that none is final or perfect. Religion is a movement, a growth; and in all true growth the new rests on the old. Every religion has in it survivals from the old. Further, even if we are not satisfied with the present forms of religion, we may anticipate a better one. If religious forms were final and infallible expressions of divine will, we should have to accept slavery, subservience of women to men and many other evils as God's work.

If we are frank, we will admit that the characters of the gods we worshipped have not been, by any means, ideal.[1] Every conceivable crime and cruelty have been attributed to the gods, though this did not interfere with the fervent worship of them by their devout followers. Even the Christian God was not very humane, if we judge by the doctrine of infant damnation, to doubt which proclaimed a man a heretic not so very long ago. It is consoling therefore to realize that no expression of religion is exhaustive and absolute. Such a belief may not help us to win the world for Buddha or for Christ, but it performs the more important task of interpreting and reconciling religious differences, and preserving religion itself from the decay which is overtaking existing systems.

Besides, Comparative Religion has been operating all along, though in an amateurish and unscientific way. Intelligent people were always aware that there were many religions which claimed control of men's lives, with their distinctive beliefs and ritual which were shaped by their distinctive environments. When the Vedic Aryans met the Dravidians and the aboriginal tribes in India, comparisons were instituted and relative merits discussed. The ancient Greeks had considerable interest in the diverse practices around them, and Herodotus has left us some observations on the beliefs and customs of the

[1] See Bernard Shaw: *The Adventures of the Black Girl in Her Search for God* (1932).

Egyptians, the Persians, the Scythians and other tribes on the fringe of barbarism. In its origin, Christianity was face to face with Judaism. Tacitus and Maximus of Tyre, some of the Gnostics, Origen and Clement, possessed knowledge of other religions. The Arab invasion of Europe confronted Christianity with Islam. The Emperor Akbar and the missionaries of every religion were in their own way exponents of Comparative Religion.[1] Only in many of these cases Comparative Religion was a branch of Apologetics, and apologists used it in defence of their respective faiths. The change which the recent study of Comparative Religion has brought about is a change equally in the spirit of approach and the exactness of the data. No longer is it impressionist pictures that we obtain, but critical estimates based on more accurate information.

IV

CHRISTIAN MISSIONS AND INDIAN FAITHS

This point may be illustrated by a reference to the delicate question of the attitude of the Christian missionaries in India to Indian faiths. This attitude has changed somewhat in the same way as have the political relations between Great Britain and India. The latter may be broadly distinguished into the three stages of (1) The East India Company, (2) The

[1] See J. E. Carpenter: *Comparative Religion* (Third Impression, 1929), chap. i.

British Empire, (3) The British Commonwealth of Nations. In the first stage, India was simply a field for exploitation. She had no rights of her own and John Company did not believe it necessary to treat her with any respect, much less reverence. The Christian missionaries of that day did not recognize anything vital or valuable in the Indian religions. For them, the native faiths were a mass of un-redeemed darkness and error. They had supreme contempt for the heathen religions and wished to root them out, lock, stock and barrel. It is a natural tendency of the human mind to suppose that its own god is God of all the earth, while all other gods are "mumbo jumbo" made with human hands. Bishop Heber's famous hymn brings out admirably this attitude of iconoclasm.[1] That Christianity is the one

[1] From Greenland's icy mountains,
    From India's coral strand,
Where Afric's sunny fountains
    Roll down their golden sand,
From many an ancient river,
    From many a palmy plain,
They call us to deliver
    Their land from error's chain.

What though the spicy breezes
    Blow soft o'er Ceylon's isle,
Though every prospect pleases
    And only man is vile!
In vain with lavish kindness
    The gifts of God are strown,
The heathen in his blindness
    Bows down to wood and stone.

[Continued on opposite page.

true religion and all other religions are utterly false has been the belief not only of the rank and file in the Christian Church but also of many Christian men and women of high intellectual standing.[1] This aggressive propaganda lacked the one thing needful —charity.

In 1858, after the Great Indian Mutiny—a mutiny was necessary—the British Government took charge of India and recognized certain rights and interests of the Indian people; but India became a dependency, a means to an end, and the interests of Great Britain were paramount. All the same, it is an improvement on the conditions of the East India Company. Similarly the Christian missionaries of the second stage realized the futility of aggressive propaganda, and did not dismiss the Indian faiths as a mass of superstition and a sink of iniquity, but regarded them as possessing some virtues of their own. For a religious development existing over forty centuries and attaining spiritual heights which challenge comparison with the best products of other

Continued from previous page.]

> Can we whose souls are lighted
>   With wisdom from on high,
> Can we to men benighted
>   The lamp of life deny?
> Salvation, O Salvation!
>   The joyful sound proclaim,
> Till each remotest nation
>   Has learnt Messiah's name.

[1] Cf. Milton's *Hymn on the Morning of Christ's Nativity.* See also Arnold Lunn: *Is Christianity True?* (1933), p. 59.

religions cannot be set aside as having no survival value. The other systems came to be regarded as a preparation, and Christianity as the crown and completion of them all. While the first attitude is reminiscent of the spirit of Tertullian, who could see in paganism nothing but the work of the devil, the second has the support of St. Paul and Origen, who recognized on every side signs of the preparation for the Gospel. St. Paul regarded the pagans as "seeking after God if haply they might find Him." His policy of being all things to all men is not the result of an ignorant opportunism. The same attitude is present in the Fourth Gospel, many of the Greek Fathers, the schoolmen of the Middle Ages and the Christian Platonists. It is argued that everything of value in the old religions is conserved in the new, for Jesus came to fulfil and not destroy. The series of volumes in *The Religious Quest of India* illustrate the second stage. But there is, right through, the imperialistic note that Christianity is the highest manifestation of the religious spirit; that it is the moral standard for the human race while every other religion is to be judged by it.

In 1917, in the middle of the War—a war was necessary; cold metal never mixes; only when thrown into the fire its hardness melts—a new conception of the relations between Great Britain and India was announced, and India was told that she would be a member of the British Commonwealth of Free Self-Governing Nations, an equal partner for imperial and international purposes. It is no more a question of exploitation as in the days of John Company, or domination as in those of the Empire, but one of free partnership. This goal is yet in the region of ideals and does not belong to the realm of achievement. The War was a great testing time for the Christian religion, which seemed to be identified during its continuance with bloodshed on a gigantic scale. A mood of self-reproach and self-criticism supervened, and the new atmosphere gave greater scope for the understanding of the spirit and value of other faiths.

The most impressive phenomenon of our times is the growing unification of the world. Science is forcing us into ever closer proximity and is weaving mankind into strange new patterns. We know every inch of the planet from Pole to Pole and our means of communication exceed the wildest dreams of our forbears. We realize that there are other worlds and other systems of thought and religion than our own. Contrasted cultures and religions are thrown together and it is difficult to shut our eyes to their vitality. Take, for example, the case of Hinduism. For many centuries its spell has bound a large part of Asia, the Middle and the Far East. With its offshoots of Buddhism, Jainism and Sikhism, it appeals to millions of people. Several militant creeds tried to suppress it, yet it is still there. Many critics ancient and modern killed it, certified its death and carried out the funeral obsequies, and yet it is there.

Men not inferior in intellect, not depraved in their
morals, not alien to the civilized in their judgments
and the values they attach to common things, men
like Gandhi and Tagore, plead guilty to being
Hindus.[1] Such a faith cannot provoke our disgust or
arouse our contempt. It kindles our curiosity. We
want to understand the sources of its strength, the
springs of its vitality. To shut our eyes to it is an
ostrich-like policy which leads nowhere. No wonder
that here and there we come across thoughtful
missionaries, none too common however, who tell
us that the future of religion consists in a free
fellowship of faiths, where by contact and exchange
each faith will acquire a new spirit and a new life.
The keynote of the new attitude is expressed by the
word "sharing." The different religious men of the
East and the West are to share their visions and
insights, hopes and fears, plans and purposes.
Unhappily, just as in the political region, so here
also this is more an aspiration than an actuality.
Comparative Religion helps us to further this ideal
of free sharing among religions which no longer
stand in uncontaminated isolation. They are regarded as different experiments influencing one
another in producing a free and creative civilization.
They are all engaged in the common effort to build
a higher and more stable life. They are fellow
workers toward the same goal. It is our duty to

[1] Cf. Sir Alfred Lyall, who said that Hinduism is determined
to live though doomed to die.

shake hands with their followers to-day and attack the forces of selfishness and stupidity, injustice and irreligion.[1]

V

THE SPIRIT OF APPROACH

Thus it is not the aim of Comparative Religion to demonstrate that this or that religion is the highest manifestation of the religious spirit. For the absoluteness of any religion is difficult to maintain when analogous phenomena are daily discovered among peoples of other faiths. The strength of the absolutist claim rests on the widespread belief that its own specific dogmas and legends are wholly unique; but Comparative Religion shows this to be erroneous. The original leaders of the study of Comparative Religion had the breadth of mind to realize this truth. God does not spurn the prayers which ascend to Him from the lips of those who do not profess our faith. Max Müller is emphatic on this point. He says: "I hold that there is a divine element in every one of the great religions of the world. I consider it blasphemous to call them the work of the devil, when they are the work of God; and I hold that there is nowhere any belief in God except as the result of a divine revelation, the effect of a divine

[1] The Report of the Appraisal Commission (1932) appointed by the Laymen's Foreign Missions Inquiry, just issued, accepts this view of the work of Christian missions as the only reasonable one for the future.

spirit working in man. I could not call myself a Christian if I were to believe otherwise, if I were to force myself against all my deepest instincts to believe that the prayers of Christians were the only prayers that God could understand. All religions are mere stammerings, our own as much as that of the Brahmins. They all have to be translated; and I have no doubt they all will be translated whatever their shortcomings may be."[1] The same attitude was adopted by Dr. Estlin Carpenter: "He would confess that he could not himself share the belief that there was any absolute form of religion. He would explain that his own studies convinced him that it was profitable to remember that Christianity is not the only form of theism or the only vehicle of moral energy that history presents and that it did not appear to him that the surviving records were adequate to justify the isolation of the Christian religion from the fraternity of human nature and normal human experience."[2] It is only when we adopt such open-mindedness that we can understand another's faith. It will remain merely a cold intellectual proposition until we make it a part of our inner being. We must experience the impression that has thrilled the follower of another faith if we wish to understand him.

The students in this college and this University

[1] *The Life and Letters of Frederick Max Müller*, vol. ii. p. 464.
[2] Weatherall: *Joseph E. Carpenter—A Memorial Volume* (1929), pp. 117–18.

are seekers of truth first and foremost. A college is not a church. It does not exist for the protection of privilege or a call to conformity. Its main function is to pursue truth in an atmosphere of freedom and fairness, even in a subject like religion where passions are easily roused. The different religions are like partners in a quest for the same objective. Your invitation to me is a proof, if proof were needed, that this college at least does not adopt an ideal lower than that of the highest freedom and truth. It does not exist for any propagandist purpose, nor can it be said that this spirit is inconsistent with the highest teaching of living faiths.

A few historical references may be given in defence of this position. The Vedic thinkers declared: "Men call him Indra, Mitra, Varuna, Agni; sages name variously him who is but one"; or again, "The sages in their hymns give many forms to him who is but one." The author of the *Bhagavadgītā* makes the teacher say: "They also who worship other gods and make offering to them with faith, O son of Kunti, do verily make offering to me, though not according to ordinance." The Buddhists insist on the same note. Aśoka's inscription at such an early hour in the history of human civilization is indeed remarkable. "The king Piyadasi honours all sects, monks and householders; he honours them by gifts and various kinds of favours. . . . For he who does reverence to his own sect while disparaging the sects of others wholly from attachment to his own, with intent to enhance the splendour of his own sect, in reality by such conduct inflicts the severest injury on his own sect."[1] Similarly the Greek thinkers developed the doctrine of the Logos as the divine reason operative in man and nature. The universality of religion is traced to the indwelling Logos. This conception played a large part in the early Christian Church. The religions are the products of "the seed of the Logos implanted in every race of men." For Justin, the Martyr (A.D. 150), those who lived with the Logos were Christians before Christ, though the fundamentalists of that age called philosophers like Socrates and Heraclitus atheists. "We have already proved Christ to be the first born of God and the Logos, of which mankind have all been partakers; and those who lived by reason were Christians notwithstanding they were thought to be atheists. Such among the Greeks were Socrates and Heraclitus and those like them." For Justin, all noble utterances in poetry or philosophy, theology or law, are derived from the discovery and contemplation of the Logos, and he could honestly say that "whatever things have been rightly said among all men are the property of us Christians."[2] All the fairest products of human thought are due to participation in the Logos. "Now of a truth I perceive that God is no respecter of persons, but in every nation, he that feareth Him and worketh righteousness is accepted

[1] Inscriptions of Aśoka: Vincent Smith: *Aśoka* (1909), p. 171.
[2] Carpenter: *Comparative Religion* (1929), p. 25.

of Him," says St. Peter. The first great Christian missionary declared that God had never left Himself without witness. When the Roman Empire brought under her sway the heterogeneous peoples of Western Asia, North Africa and Southern and Middle Europe, her thinkers discovered the oneness of God as the common link binding together the different worships. Eusebius of Caesarea (about A.D. 260–340) wrote a treatise entitled *The Preparation for the Gospel* which Dr. Estlin Carpenter called "the first great work on comparative religion which issued out of Christian theology."[1] "There is one Supreme God," wrote Maximus of Madaura to Augustine about A.D. 390, "without natural offspring, who is, as it were, the God and Mighty Father of all. The powers of the Deity, diffused through the universe which He has made, we worship under many names, as we are all ignorant of His true name. Thus it happens that while in diverse supplications we approach separated, as it were, certain parts of the Divine Being, we are seen in reality to be the worshippers of Him in whom all these parts are one."[2] Even Augustine, who is regarded as the champion of dogmatic Christianity, in his last book (*Retractationes*) says: "The very thing which is now called the Christian religion existed among the ancients, and never failed from the beginning of the human race up to the coming of Christ in the flesh. Then the true religion which already existed began to be

[1] Carpenter: *Comparative Religion*, p. 53.   [2] Ibid., p. 35.

called Christianity."[1] The Emperor Akbar who, according to Max Müller, "may be considered the first who ventured on a comparative study of the religions of the world,"[2] was led to give up his faith in the absoluteness of Islam and declare that "there are sensible men in all religions and abstemious thinkers and men endowed with miraculous powers among all nations." There are prayers to Varuṇa in the Rig Veda which recall the language of the Psalms and of the Christian literature of devotion. The devotees of God in ancient Babylon or Egypt, or in our Rome and Benares, draw near the throne of mercy with the same words of yearning and praise, confession and prayer. In essence, the inner religious consciousness has altered little. It finds for itself different modes of expression, and historical circumstances account for these variations. To the understanding eye the things that unite are greater than those that divide.

When properly studied, Comparative Religion increases our confidence in the universality of God and our respect for the human race. It induces in us not an attitude of mere tolerance which implies conscious superiority, not patronizing pity, not condescending charity, but genuine respect and appreciation.[3] We should try to discover in every

[1] I. 13.

[2] *Introduction to the Science of Religion* (1909), Appendix to chap. i. p. 68.

[3] Max Müller overshot the mark when he said: "No other religion, with the exception perhaps of early Buddhism, would

sincere and earnest teacher of things divine, whether ancient or modern, "what the spirit which was in them did signify."[1] It is no use studying the world's religions as archaeologists do the ruins of a vanished past preserved in a museum of antiquities. For they represent the aspirations of the human mind after a life which is not of this world, aspirations which are not mere dreams but the most powerful realities in men's lives. If then there are striking resemblances among the different religions, they may be due to their common origin, or to the fact that when faced by the same phenomena human intelligence drew similar inferences, and led by common instincts built up similar cults.

VI

PROBLEMS OF COMPARATIVE RELIGION

The subject of Comparative Religion includes a number of distinct problems. The circumstances

have favoured the idea of an impartial comparison of the principal religions of the world. . . . It is Christianity alone, which, as the religion of humanity, as the religion of no caste, of no chosen people, has taught us to study the history of mankind as our own, to discover the traces of a divine wisdom and love in the development of all the races of the world and to recognize, if possible, even in the lowest and crudest forms of religious beliefs not the work of the devil, but something that indicates a divine guidance." *Introduction to the Science of Religion*, p. 29.

[1] I Peter i. 2.

attending its commencement account for the emphasis which is generally laid on questions of religious origins. Other religions are studied with an anthropological or antiquarian interest, whether they arose out of the cults of the dead or were born of dread and desire to keep the malignant powers at a distance. We reach a period of time where conjecture takes the place of evidence. I do not wish to minimize the importance of these studies, but my main concern in this course is not with these questions.

There are again problems about the history of the different religions. Ingenious theories attempt to prove that Ahuramazda of Zoroastrianism and Ashur are one, that Abraham, Aaron and Arthur are "allotropic forms of the same element." Sir James Frazer compares the myth of Adonis as it existed in Babylonia, from whom Greece borrowed it in the seventh century B.C., with the corresponding myth of Attis in Phrygia and the similar legends of Osiris in Egypt.[1] Jensen spread the story and supported it by an extraordinary amount of clever and difficult trifling that Moses, Jesus and Paul were only variations on Gilgamesh, the mythical hero of the old Babylonian epic. The belief in the death and the rising again of gods is found in Egypt, Babylonia, Phoenicia and Syria, and a good deal of information about it can be found in a large volume of *The Golden Bough* bearing the title *The*

[1] See his book on *Adonis, Attis and Osiris* (1906).

Dying God. The relation of primitive Christianity to the Mystery religions of the early Roman Empire is worked out by Professor Kirsopp Lake in his book on *Paul's Earlier Epistles.* The birth stories of Buddha, Krishna and Jesus have certain striking resemblances suggestive of mutual borrowing. The similarities in the teachings of the Bhagavadgītā and the Gospels have led some to think that Krishna and Christ were one. A comparison of the lives of the founders of the two religions of Buddhism and Christianity, their scriptures and their ethical teachings is undoubtedly an instructive study. The study of the ancestry of ideas is a fertile branch of Comparative Religion.

Whatever may be the value of this or that speculation, the comparative method when used with imagination and restraint, with sympathy and reverence, will help us to see the common background of the different religions and their composite character, and impress on us the unity as much as the multitudinousness of human nature. We may select any two faiths and study their foundational motives and broad features, or compare particular aspects like mysticism, asceticism, sacrifice, prayer, incarnation, etc. From such investigations it would be possible for us to obtain results of the greatest importance. We can ascertain which of the elements of a religion are native to it and which borrowed and from whom, and whether the resemblances are superficial or deep rooted. Are the agreements due to suggestions arising from historical contact, or are they derived from certain common types of experience?[1] What forces of thought have shaped them and what feelings do they express? Again, how is it that peoples belonging to a common stock profess different religions? What are the effects of climate, contacts with other peoples and struggle with environment? Comparative Religion, by a study of these parallels and analogies, broadens our vision. When we criticize myths and miracles in other religions, the same attitude of discriminating criticism should be extended to our own.

If we trace the successive forms of change and the steps through which a religion has progressed, if we wish to go behind the external evolution of a given religion, its modes of worship and its doctrines, we must face the more difficult questions of the causes which shaped these acts and moulded these beliefs. These lead us to a third set of problems, different from the anthropological or the historical, viz. the philosophical. Here we confront the questions of value and of validity. How far can the facts gathered by Comparative Religion be accepted as expressing the reality of an unseen ground? If we leave out of account those forms of worship and belief which we find among the primitive and unsettled races, who

[1] Some modern anthropologists are not so much inclined to accept the view that coincidences may be due to the deeper unity of man and nature. They are more in favour of the diffusion hypothesis.

do not possess any holy texts or sacred laws or even hymns and prayers which are handed down from one generation to another, the historical religions happen to be seven or eight. The Semitic races are responsible for three, the Jewish, the Christian and the Mohammedan faiths. Hinduism with its many offshoots of Buddhism, Jainism and Sikhism, and Zoroastrianism are developed by the Aryan races. These together with the systems of Confucius and Laotze form the living faiths of mankind. It is not possible in this course, even if I had the competence, to deal with the higher thought of these faiths. It shall be my endeavour to consider with you the presuppositions of the religious experience of mankind as it exists in one or two of its reflective forms in a spirit of good will, comparing "spiritual things with spiritual," as St. Paul says.[1] As men of religion it is our duty to recognize and rejoice in truth and goodness wherever we find them in the assurance that all that is true and good is from God.

VII

METHOD OF TREATMENT

For one thing Comparative Religion has rendered untenable the usual distinction between religions of true and false. The universal condemnation, pronounced by the Roman Catholic and the Anglican

[1] I Cor. ii. 13.

articles on non-Christian faiths as "all false," becomes absurd. Generally the distinction between true and false is identical with mine and thine. It answers to the distinction between Jew and Gentile, Hindu and Mleccha, Greek and barbarian, Christian and heathen, Moslem and Kaffir. This dichotomy is useless for our purposes.

The contrast between revealed and natural religion, though not identical with that between the true and the false, is used to imply the latter. Revealed religion occupies a privileged position. Revelation is a universal gift, not a parochial possession. We can no longer say that truth has found its home in one part of the world alone. We are able to realize more vividly than did our forefathers that God has made Himself known to men in diverse manners. We no more assume that all that is good and true and valuable is found in any one religion, while those who do not chance to adopt it are doomed to everlasting pain. Such religious chauvinism would sound very strange on our lips. We have now a nobler and truer view of God.

With regard to religions, therefore, the question is not of truth or falsehood but life or death. Is it a dead curiosity or a going concern? Every living religion has its part in the spiritual education of the race. Many of our religious paradoxes and perplexities are due to the narrowness of our horizon. By enlarging our sympathies we raise our thought above the narrow controversies of the day. We are all familiar with Goethe's paradox: "He who knows one language knows none." The poet asked "What does he know of England who only England knows?" What is true of language and history is true of religion also. We cannot understand our own religion unless it be in relation to one or more of the other faiths. By an intelligent and respectful study of other religions we gain a new understanding and appreciation of their traditions and our own. Anything which contributes to this growth of harmony of thought deserves to be encouraged. Comparative Religion is one of the chief instruments by which the historic consciousness of the spiritual growth of mankind can be gained.

Again, India happens to be intimately related with Great Britain, and if the bonds are to be more enduring than material links, a better understanding of the religions of India is necessary. Some of the leaders of thought in this country—the late Lord Haldane and Principal Jacks—are aware of this need. In an article on *East and West* which Lord Haldane contributed to the *Hibbert Journal*[1] a few weeks before his death, he insisted on the new "task of learning to govern India through a mutual understanding and sympathy, which may carry us a long way towards the solution of a problem which seems insoluble only because we have made it so." "Has not the time come," asks Principal Jacks, "when it behoves the leaders of the Church to

[1] July 1928.

recognize that the State has in India alone some three hundred millions of non-Christian subjects whose religious liberty it guarantees, and that the mind of the State in consequence has to view its duties to religion in a much wider perspective than that of any controversy among contending sections of the Established Church, or indeed, of any controversy whatsoever which turns exclusively on the internal differences of the Christian religion?" For any religious internationalism, a study of Comparative Religion is the indispensable basis. It gives the foundations, which cannot be overthrown, of all religions. It is essential to-day when religious thought has reached a distinctive stage in its development which alarmists characterize as a crisis.

LECTURE II

EAST AND WEST IN RELIGION

LECTURE II

EAST AND WEST IN RELIGION[1]

I

CONTACT BETWEEN EAST AND WEST

To deal with this vast subject with any approach
to adequacy in a single lecture is impossible. I can
refer only to a few major considerations regarding
the distinctive outlooks associated with the two
great currents of humanity, the Asiatic and the
European. In the history of human culture Asia
and Europe represent two complementary sides;
Asia the spiritual and Europe the intellectual.
Occasionally the two streams met with mutual
advantage. In the first instance Eastern wisdom,
the Egyptian, the Chaldean and the Indian, influenced Western philosophers like Pythagoras and
Plato. Alexander's invasion of Western Asia and the
Buddhist Missions to Syria and Palestine in the
centuries before the Christian era may be regarded
as marking the second contact. From one of Aśoka's
inscriptions, we learn that in the early part of the
third century B.C., Buddhist missions were sent to
the court of the Seleucidæ at Antioch and the court
of the Ptolemies at Alexandria. The invasion of

[1] The Jowett lecture given on March 18, 1930, at the Mary
Ward Settlement, London.

43

Spain and the southern coast of the Mediterranean by the followers of Islam is the third attempt. The extent and the manner in which these three meetings influenced the great Greco-Roman, the Christian and the modern civilizations are difficult to determine. The most hopeful fact about the future of humanity is the present bringing together of the peoples of the world. East and West can no longer be isolated either in thought or in life. Contacts between them which were hitherto occasional and brief have now become steady and permanent.

II

THE NEED FOR RELIGION

The unity of the modern world demands a new cultural basis; and the real issue is whether it is to be guided by the economic and the pragmatistic mind, which is the more dominant at the moment, or by the spiritual. A mechanical world in which humanity is welded into a machine of soulless efficiency is not the proper goal for human endeavour. We need a spiritual outlook which will include in its intention not only the vast surging life of economics and politics but the profound needs of the soul. The real character of a civilization is to be gathered not so much from its forms and institutions as from the values of the spirit, the furniture of the mind. Religion is the inside of a civilization, the

44

soul as it were of the body of its social organization. Scientific applications, economic alliances, political institutions may bring the world together outwardly; but for a strong and stable unity the invisible but deeper bonds of ideas and ideals require to be strengthened. In the work of rebuilding the human household, the *rôle* of religion is no less important than that of science. The human individual consists of body, mind and spirit. Each requires its proper nutriment. The body is kept trim by food and exercise, the mind is informed by science and criticism, and the spirit is illumined by art and literature, philosophy and religion. If the spirit of humanity is to grow it can only be by the exercise of its lovelier energies. The Asiatic and the European streams have achieved marvellous results each in its own way, the former by its absolute spiritual sincerity and the latter by its severe intellectual integrity. The great stream of life carves out its bed for itself according to the slope of the region traversed. The relatively independent existence of the two continents in thought and life has led to certain specific characteristics and forms. But, of course, there are no qualities of mind and spirit which are the exclusive possession of any one race. The great peoples differ not so much in the presence or absence of this or that quality as in its degree or extent. The West is not devoid of mysticism and martyrdom nor the East of science and public spirit. The distinction, if any, is a relative one, as

45

all empirical distinctions are. If then there is appearance of dogmatism in what I shall say, it is due simply to the convenience of exposition. For while dogmatists and narrow nationalists distinguish in order to divide, a seeker of truth divides only to distinguish.

III

LIVING RELIGIONS

In the matter of religion, India typifies the East. Geographically it is between the Semitic West and the Mongolian East. The late Mr. Lowes Dickinson in his *Essay on the Civilizations of India, China and Japan* observed that India is the only country that typifies the East. The Semitic spirit is more akin to the Western in its activism and love of power. Having been a close neighbour of Rome, Semitic Asia cultivated the spirit of combat and organization. It is the twilight region between the East and the West. Again, in the Far East the Eastern mysticism glides slowly into love of beauty and order and a spirit of pragmatism. Greece and Rome typify the spirit of the West.

Among living religions, still further, there is none which has a Western origin. They have all been cradled in India, Iran or Palestine. Some of them spread to the West. Thus Christianity is an Eastern religion, transplanted into the West where it acquired

46

forms characteristic of the Western mind. Hinduism and Buddhism are confined to the East. Judaism was subjected to pronounced Western influence in the days of the Alexandrian School. In pre-Christian times the Jews of Alexandria came into touch with Greek life and thought. The Judaeo-Alexandrian School of religious philosophy, of which Philo was the last great representative, is the outcome of this contact. Islam grew out of Judaism and is largely indebted to the Greeks and the Spaniards in the West. In the tenth and eleventh centuries which were the golden period of Islamic culture, the Greek works of science and philosophy were familiar in Arabic, and the great revolution in thought produced in the twelfth and thirteenth centuries was due to the arrival in Europe of a number of Latin translations of Arabic works. Yet Judaism and Islam remain predominantly oriental. While Hinduism and Buddhism may be regarded as typically Eastern, since they are so both in origin and in development, Christianity may be taken as the type of the Western religion. For it is a law of life that religions like other things take on the nature of the organisms which assimilate them. The distinction between the pure and simple teaching of Jesus and the developments Christianity assumed in the West is a striking illustration of the difference between the Eastern and the Western attitudes to religion.

IV

SPIRITUAL LIFE AND INTELLECTUAL
FORMALISM

The Western mind is rationalistic and ethical, posi-
tivist and practical, while the Eastern mind is more
inclined to inward life and intuitive thinking.
Robert Bridges in *The Testament of Beauty* says that
in the past the West looked to the East for spiritual
wisdom, and the East is now dazzled by the material
conquests of the West.

> Our fathers travelled eastward to revel in wonders
> Where pyramid, pagoda and picturesque attire
> Glow in the fading sunset of antiquity;
> And now will the orientals make hither in return
> Outlandish pilgrimage; their wiseacres have seen
> The electric light in the west, and come to worship;
> Tasting romance in our unsightly novelties
> And scientific tricks; for all things in their day
> May have opinion of glory. Glory is opinion,
> The vain doxology wherewith man would praise God.[1]

Speaking in general terms we may say that the
dominant feature of Eastern thought is its insistence
on creative intuition, while the Western systems are
characterized by a greater adherence to critical
intelligence.[2] The living, the concrete, the individual, is distinct from the merely logical. Logic tends

[1] I, 589–598.
[2] See the writer's Hibbert Lectures on *An Idealist View of Life*
(1932), chap. iv.

to reduce everything to identity, but there is nothing
that remains the same for two successive moments
of its existence. Intellect seeks to congeal the flowing
stream in blocks of ice. Truth is something that is
lived and not merely logically comprehended, and
yet we need logic in order to think, prove and
communicate our ideas and perceptions. While the
East believes that there are realities which cannot
be clearly seen, and even assumes that logical
attempts to formulate them in communicable propositions do violence to them, the West demands
clearness and is shy of mystery. What is expressed
and is useful for our immediate ends is real, what
is inexpressible and useless is unreal. It has been
well said: "The Greeks with all their acuteness and
skill had little real religious instinct. In this respect
the more practical West and the more mystical
East have always diverged."[1] Plato's sympathy with
mysticism shows how very far removed he is from
the ordinary Greek.[2]

There is an anxiety for definition and form in
the Western religions. The Greek spirit is not satisfied with the conception of the supreme as a spiritual
reality, or an abstract power or a shadowy force
immanent in the world. It must give to its gods
concrete natures with definite physical traits. Eros,
for example, is a beautiful personal God. The

[1] Article "Jesus Christ" by Dr. Stanley Cook, *Encyclopaedia
Britannica*, 14th ed., 1929.
[2] See Earp: *The Way of the Greeks* (1929), p. 47.

anthropomorphism of the Greek mind is well known.[1] Its "concretizing" nature is responsible for its clothing its gods in as definite forms as the visible and tangible embodiments in the works of plastic art.[2] The great insistence on the personality of God in the Christian religion is an inheritance from Greek intellectualism.

An intellectual religion confuses pictures with proofs, mysteries with dogmas. For it, the objects of knowledge are ever the same, unvarying myth and symbol are only masks. It trades on words and misses their meaning.[3] Absolutism results with its corollary of organization on the basis of a creed or a ritual. An organized religion or a church is hostile to every belief which is opposed to its own creed. If new knowledge threatens the old creeds, it is the knowledge that suffers. A church cannot allow liberty of thought within its borders or, for that matter, even without. It is obliged to enforce beliefs and persecute unbelief on principle. If the fair name

[1] Cf. Dr. Farnell: "Of the Hellenic religion no feature is so salient as its anthropomorphism, and throughout its whole development and career the anthropomorphic principle has been more dominating and imperious than it has ever been found to be in other religions." *Greece and Babylon* (1911), p. 11.
[2] Cornford: *Greek Religious Thought* (1923), p. xii.
[3] Mephistopheles says of Theology: "Generally speaking, stick to words; you will then pass through the safe gate into the temple of certainty." When the student suggests that "there must be some meaning connected with the word," Mephistopheles replies, "Right: only we must not be too anxious about that; for it is precisely where meaning fails

of Greece is not stained by any religious wars, it was due to its polytheism. The Greeks do not insist that if we call Zeus by some other name, we will suffer eternal perdition.

In the East religion is more the life of spirit. It is the perception of the oneness of man with the spirit of truth, love and beauty in the universe. Such a view does not exaggerate the *rôle* of intellectual propositions. It admits them as timid efforts at simplifying the real. It is convinced of the inexhaustibility of the divine and the infinite number of its possible manifestations. There is a "beyond" of expression into which no expression reaches, though it animates all expressions and lends them substance and significance. Centuries before Israel and the psalms of David we hear the supplication of a nameless Egyptian poet who addresses God not as friend or saviour, not as made in man's image or symbol enshrined in stone. "He is not seen; He hath neither minister nor offerings; He is not worshipped in temples; His dwelling is not known. No shrine of His hath painted images. There is no habitation which may hold Him. Unknown is His name in heaven, and His form is not manifested, for every image of Him is in vain. His home is in the universe, not in any dwelling made

that a word comes in most opportunely. Disputes may be admirably carried on with words; a system may be built with words; words form a capital subject for belief; a word admits not an iota being taken from it."

51

by human hands." Religious forms are not so much true as significant. Meaning cannot be measured by external standards. To appreciate the meaning of a religious idea or symbol, we must find out the value it expresses and achieves. The spirit is not tied to any form however adequate. Eastern religions are non-dogmatic and their adherents possess as a rule what may be called spiritual good manners. They do not condemn the good simply because it is not the best. They respect the individual as he is and do not insist on improving him even when he is unwilling. In heaven there are not only many mansions but also many vehicles to reach them. The Hindu and the Buddhist religions recognize every form of faith as a possessor of some degree of truth, with the doubtful result that all sorts of foreign cults and superstitious beliefs are to be found within the pale of these religions.

A natural consequence of this difference in emphasis is that in the East religion is more a matter of spiritual culture than of scholastic learning. We learn the truth not by criticism and discussion but by deepening life and changing the level of consciousness. God is not the highest form to be known but the highest being to be realized. Passive virtues are emphasized, like the meditative calm and the strength of spirit which are the outcome of self-control and waging war on lust, anger and worry. Religion is the dominant thing in life, its light and law. Sheik Abdullah Ansar of Herat used to tell his pupils: "To fly in the air is no miracle, for the dirtiest flies can do it; to cross rivers without bridge or boat is no miracle, for a terrier can do the same; but to help suffering hearts is a miracle performed by holy men." Eastern religions lay stress on the patience of spirit and the gentleness of soul which are born not of fear but of strength which refuses to push its way in a crowd.

V

QUIETISM VERSUS ACTIVISM

Vigorous life and active service appeal to the West. Life is a thing to be possessed and enjoyed. The part of wisdom is to make the most of it and order it to the best purpose, instead of looking vainly beyond to some unknown, unattainable, infinite satisfaction. The life force manifests itself in the visible universe and man is the meaning of the cosmic process. The free power of the individual self and the organized will of the corporate community are the great upbuilding forces. The development of individual personality interpreted humanistically and national efficiency are the ideal ends. Virtue is conformity to custom. It is a sense of fitness or decorum, preserving appearances, respecting public opinion. The golden mean is a Greek contribution to ethical theory. Excess in all things is to be deprecated, whether in the matter of pleasure or power, wealth or wisdom. Rashness is a vice as much as cowardice, asceticism as much as indulgence. To the Greek piety is prudence.

Religion in the East is the cultivation of the interior life. It is the attainment of spiritual freedom, and is essentially the private achievement of the individual won by hard effort in solitude and isolation, on mountain-tops and in monasteries. The calm and compassion of a Buddha victorious over suffering, the meditation of the thinker in communion with the eternal, the rapture of the devotee in love with the transcendent, the dedication of the saint raised above egoistic desires and passions into the selflessness of the divine possess value to the Eastern mind higher than a life of power and enjoyment.

In the West, religion is a social phenomenon, a matter of the ecclesia, of the community. The Greek morality was essentially tribal. The Greek acknowledged duties to those who were bound to him by special ties, but to the rest of mankind, to man as man, he owed only the common obligations that were imposed by the feeling of decency. Religion in the West is a support for social stability and a shield against the innovator. Gods are the promoters of the social customs. Ceremonies which bind the groups are emphasized. Good citizens are good believers and those who break the rules are atheists. Naturally the State becomes a Church and its saviours obtain religious veneration. Hercules and Theseus were deified men. Divine honours were paid to Scipio Africanus and the image of Julius Caesar was carried in the solemn procession of the gods. Roman emperors were admitted to the pantheon after their death. The great funeral speech of Pericles, which may be regarded as the expression of the highest religion of the Greeks, contains no reference to the Greek gods. To fight for Athens is to fight for Athene. In the great battle against the Thebans, Theseus encourages his men, according to Euripides, thus: "O sons of Athens! if ye cannot stay the stubborn spear of the men sprung from the dragon's teeth, the cause of Pallas is overthrown."[1] Dr. Farnell observes: "No other religion of which we have any record was so political as the Hellenic."[2] All cults which favour social harmony are tolerated. Gibbon tells us in his *Decline and Fall of the Roman Empire* that the Roman magistrates "encouraged the public festivals which humanize the manners of the people. They managed the arts of divination as convenient instruments of policy, and they respected as the firmest bond of society the useful persuasion that either in this or a future life the crime of perjury is most assuredly punished by the avenging gods. But whilst they acknowledged the general advantages of religion they were convinced that the various modes of worship contributed alike to the same salutary purposes and that in every country the form of superstition, which had received the sanction of time and experience,

[1] Farnell: *The Higher Aspects of Greek Religion* (1912), p. 80.
[2] *Greece and Macedon* (1911), p. 21.

was the best adapted to the climate and its inhabitants." The Greek tolerance is the result of political opportunism and is not a considered conviction. The polytheism of the Greeks and their political sense were their security against intolerance. If a Socrates is persecuted it is because of his danger to the State. Religion in the West becomes confused with a sort of mystical nationalism. The universal element dominates the Eastern religions.

The ahimsā of the Upaniṣads and the love and compassion of the Buddha enfold even the lowest forms of animal life within their merciful arms. There is a tendency to otherworldliness in Eastern religions, while this-worldliness is a characteristic of Western types. Eastern religions aim at producing saints and heroes: Western, men that are sensible and happy. The Eastern religions are directed to the salvation of the individual soul rather than to the maintenance of society. The Western convert religion into a sort of police system for the sake of social order. The great men of the East, Buddha, Jesus, Mohammed, swung the world into a new orbit and wrought inward changes. Their legacy is interwoven into the fabric of men's minds. Caesar, Cromwell and Napoleon are men of the world: they are content to work with the material ready to their hands and reduce it to order and decency. They teach no new way of life and they bring no comfort to the weary and the sick at heart. And yet our social institutions bear the impress of their work.

We have in the West the realism of the men of action: in the East the sensitiveness of the artist and imagination of the creative dreamer. The ideal of Western culture, derived from Greek philosophy, is to train men for citizenship that they may be able to realize their full power in the State and for the State. In the East, the good man is one who feels at home in the whole world. Both types are essential, for no spiritual revelation can flourish in an anarchical society.

Emphasis on logical reason, humanist ideals, social solidarity and national efficiency are the characteristic marks of the Western attitude to life. The outstanding epochs of Western culture—the Greek age, the Roman world before Constantine, the period of the Renaissance and our own times—bear witness to the great tradition founded on reason and science, on ordered knowledge of the powers and possibilities of physical nature, and of man conceived as a psycho-physical organism, on an ordered use of that knowledge for a progressive social efficiency and well-being which will make the brief life of man more easy and comfortable.

VI

THE RELIGION OF JESUS AND WESTERN CHRISTIANITY

The difference between the Eastern and the Western approaches and attitudes to religion becomes evi-

dent when we compare the life of Jesus, and His
teaching as recorded in the Gospels, with the Nicene
Creed. It is the difference between a type of personality and a set of dogmas, between a way of life
and a scheme of metaphysics. The characteristics
of intuitive realization, non-dogmatic toleration, as
well as insistence on the non-aggressive virtues and
universalist ethics, mark Jesus out as a typical
Eastern seer. On the other hand, the emphasis on
definite creeds and absolutist dogmatism, with its
consequences of intolerance, exclusiveness and confusion of piety with patriotism, are the striking
features of Western Christianity.

Jesus' religion was one of love and sympathy,
tolerance and inwardness. He founded no organization but enjoined only private prayer. He was
utterly indifferent to labels and creeds. He made
no distinction between Jew and Gentile, Roman
and Greek. He did not profess to teach a new
religion but only deepened spiritual life. He for-
mulated no doctrine and did not sacrifice thinking
to believing. He learned and taught in the syna-
gogues of the Jews. He observed their ritual so long
as it did not blind men to the inner light. He
attached no importance to professions of allegiance.
There is nothing in common between the simple
truths taught by Jesus and the Church militant with
its hierarchic constitution and external tests of
membership. But the change was inevitable when
Christianity went to Rome and took over the

58

traditions of Caesar. When the Greek dialecticians and the Roman lawyers succeeded to the Jewish divines and the prophets, Christian theology became logical in form and based on law. The spirit was the Jew's but the letter or the dogma was the Greek's, and the polity and the organization were the Roman's.[1] Jesus reveals through His life and commends through His teaching the possibility of a life of a higher quality than that which is normal to man. He does not discuss intricacies of theology and ritual, but proclaims love of God or insight

[1] Dr. Hatch observes: "It shows itself mainly in three ways: (i) The first of them was the tendency to define. The earliest Christians had been content to believe in God and to woiship Him without endeavouring to define precisely the conception of Him which lay beneath their faith and their worship. They thought of Him as one, as beneficent, and as supreme. But they drew no fence of words round their idea of Him, and still less did they attempt to demonstrate by processes of reason that their idea of Him was true. (ii) The second manifestation of the philosophical habit of mind was the tendency to speculate, that is, to draw inferences from definitions, to weave the inferences into systems and to test assertions by their logical consistency or inconsistency with those systems. The earliest Christians had but little conception of a system. The inconsistency of one apparently true statement with another did not vex their souls. Their beliefs reflected the variety of the world and of men's thoughts about the world. (iii) The holding of approved opinions was elevated to a position at first co-ordinate with, and at last superior to, trust in God and the effort to live a holy life." Hatch: *The Influence of the Greek Ideas and Usages upon the Christian Church* (1890), pp. 135-7. Cf. Harnack: "Dogma in its conception and development is a work of the Greek spirit on the soil of the gospel." *History of Dogma*, vol. i. p. 17 (1896).

into the nature of reality, and love of man or oneness with the purpose of the universe, as the central
truths of religion. Transplanted into the West, creeds
and dogmas took the place of vision and prophecy,
and intricate subtleties of scholasticism displaced
the simple love of God. The question for the Church
is not whether the ideas it represents are spiritually
worthy, but what are the ways and means by which
the society can be held together. Roman ideas and
institutions influenced the ecclesiastical organization.

VII

THE INCARNATION AND THE TRINITY

For Jesus piety is not a matter of knowledge, nor is
ignorance the cause of impiety. His simple faith
appealed to the uncultured peasants. Celsus sarcas-
tically declared that the law of admission to the
Christian communities was: "Let no educated man
enter, no wise man, no prudent man, for such things
we deem evil; but whoever is ignorant, whoever is
unintelligent, whoever is uneducated, whoever is
simple, let him come and be welcome." Tertullian
asked, "What resemblance is there between a
philosopher and a Christian, between a disciple
of Greece and a disciple of heaven?"[1] And yet
this simple faith, which seems to be so radically

[1] Hatch: *The Influence of the Greek Ideas and Usages upon the Christian Church* (1890), pp. 124 and 134.

opposed to the Greek temperament, when taken over by the Greeks is transformed into a theological scheme.

The Greeks and Romans were interested in God as a theoretical explanation of the universe. The relation of the infinite to the finite was the outstanding problem of Greek philosophy, and the solutions offered by Plato and Aristotle were ambiguous and unsatisfactory. The incarnation theory offered a way out. God is no longer separated by a meaningless distance from the human world, but has actually entered into humanity, thus making possible the ultimate unity of the human race with God. In Jesus we have the union of the divine and the human. The spaceless spirit has penetrated the world of sense. The Nicene Creed is an answer to a problem of Greek metaphysics and not of Jewish religion. Since its formulation there have been many doctrinal controversies.

We notice also the gradual transformation of a rigid monotheism into a trinitarian Godhead. The Greeks worshipped not merely Father Zeus but a whole society of gods and goddesses. In Greco-Latin paganism Zeus was conceived as Jupiter and as the head of all the gods and goddesses who shared his divinity. When pagan polytheism and Jewish monotheism became fused together, the Catholic God, a God who is a society, arose. The Roman Emperors, keen on dissolving the distinction between the citizenship of the State and membership of the Church, took up the local deities and converted them into Christian saints.

The Roman Empire failed to destroy Christianity by persecution, but the hour of her victory over Rome signalized the defeat of the gospel of Jesus. Christianity became bound up with the civilization under which it grew. The Church became the depository of sacred wisdom, a sort of reservoir of theological secrets and not a spring.

Christianity is a syncretistic faith, a blend of various earlier creeds. The Jew, the Greek and the Roman as well as the races of the Mediterranean basin have contributed to it, with the result that, in spite of its anxiety for system, this is lacking. Its ideas about God, to take one example, vary between a loving father, a severe judge, a detective officer, a hard schoolmaster and the head of the clerical profession.

VIII

HOSPITALITY OF EARLY CHRISTIANITY AND ITS ABSENCE IN LATER CHRISTIANITY

When once religious faith becomes confused with dogmatic creeds, exclusiveness and intolerance become inevitable. Christianity in its early form was quite hospitable to Western thought and beliefs with which it came into contact. The Fourth Gospel adopted the doctrine of the Logos and took up the position that those who worshipped Christ were not setting up a new god. The Fourth Evangelist was not troubled by the fact that the Logos doctrine was Greek in origin and had heathen associations. No canons of orthodoxy bound him to a narrow Jewish faith. Justin Martyr could say: "The teachings of Plato are not alien to those of Christ, though not in all respects similar. For all the writers were able to have a dim vision of realities by means of the indwelling seed of the implanted word."[1] And yet in the fourth century Christianity developed an attitude of intolerance. The great library at Alexandria founded by the first Ptolemy in the third century B.C. and lavishly endowed by his successors was finally destroyed under the orders of the Christian emperor Theodosius the Great in A.D. 389, because it was known to be a hotbed of paganism.[2] A few centuries later, when Christianity came into contact with Islam, it did not adopt the liberal attitude of the earlier stage and try to find out the elements of truth in Islam, but fought it bitterly and bigotedly. Even if we admit that Islam is a militant organization, a fighting brotherhood in which a rigorous discipline is imposed on its followers by means of the scripture of the Quran and the organs of interpretation, we cannot deny that the conception of brotherhood in Islam transcends all barriers of race and nationality, a feature which does not charac-

[1] *Apology*, ii. 13.
[2] It is true that it was partly ruined by the army of Julius Caesar during the siege of Alexandria.

terize many other religions. To-day when Christianity is faced by the religion of India,[1] it is adopting an attitude of unbending self-sufficiency. It has lost the features of teachability and tolerance which characterized it in its early days.

It has ceased to be a religion of growth and freedom and become one of regimentation. The Church is the bearer of the revelation and only the revelation, not the Church, is authoritative. The prophetic element is authoritative and not its formulations. The Church formulates dogma in terms of the current thought, but she cannot claim absolute intellectual finality for any dogma or formula. The thinking of the past in no way renders unnecessary the thinking of the present. The contrast between the free and simple religion of Jesus, and the dogmatic system of the Church, is brought out in the Chapter on "The Grand Inquisitor" in Dostoevsky's book *The Brothers Karamazov*. The Grand Inquisitor explains to Jesus that the Church has undone his work, corrected it and refounded it on the basis of authority. The souls of men were indeed like sheep and could not endure the terrible gift of freedom which Jesus had brought. The Church has been merciful in keeping man from knowledge and free inquiry. It has made mental slaves of its members. Belief is heaven and heresy hell. Consider the

[1] "Far more ancient than that of the Greeks, far more enduring, far more spiritual." Hoyland: *The Cross moves East* (1931), p. 63.

repressive legislation of Theodosius, which by heavy penalties forbade the practice of any other religion than Christianity, the closing of the schools of philosophy at Athens by Justinian, the Albigensian Crusades, the Dominican Inquisitions, the Acts of Supremacy and Uniformity in Elizabethan England, the religious wars of the seventeenth century and the cruelties perpetrated upon the anabaptists. Pius IX declared, "Let us most firmly hold that according to Catholic doctrine, there is one God, one Faith, one Baptism, and to go further (in an enquiry as to the fate of souls) were sin." Even those philosophers who profess to be devotees of truth are unable to shake themselves free from the absolutism characteristic of intellectual religions. While they admit that the Christian religion is not the only one, they believe that it is the absolute expression of absolute truth. In it we have the thrusting of the eternal into the temporal. As Hegel says: "It is the Christian religion which is the perfect religion, the religion which represents the Being of Spirit in a realized form or for itself, the religion in which religion has itself become objective in relation to itself."[1] But if we are true to the teaching of Jesus, we shall know that absolute truth goes beyond all forms and creeds, all historic revelations and institutions.

[1] *Philosophy of Religion*, E.T. (1895), vol. ii. p. 330.

IX

NATIONALIST BIAS

Jesus wants us to make religion the light and law of our life. He substituted an ethical ideal for ceremonial duties. "A broken and contrite heart" counts for more than outer conformity, which is a vain and barren thing without the vitalizing sense of God. Jesus denounced Pharisees who sought to buy peace with heaven a little too cheaply. The call of God takes precedence of the claims of fathers and mothers, wives and children. But we are unwilling to make religion the shaping power of our lives. We take it with Greek "moderation." The saints are generally creatures set apart, those who flee from the temporal world to seek the reality of God. They live in prayer and devotion. Solitude and isolation are the roots of their existence. Those deeply influenced by the spirit of Jesus even in the West, feed the deer, hold converse with the stars, and if they are men of action they heal the sick and preach the word of God. They are not anxious for popular applause or social approbation.

The practice of the principles of Jesus will mean a society of all mankind, a society in which we bear one another's burdens and sympathize with each other in joy and sorrow. Such a society will be free from national rivalries and industrial competitions, since it will attach little importance to external goods in which one man's gain is another's loss; but we are unwilling to adopt such a view of ethics.

Jesus warns us that it is of no avail if we gain the whole world and lose our soul, if we buy peace with the world at the cost of our convictions. Inward truthfulness and spiritual sincerity are essential. To-day the religious hero is not so much a being near to God as a servant of the nation. St. Joan was clear that he who attacked France attacked God. She announced that France was always right, France was always with God, and to oppose France was to oppose Right and God. Christianity is associated with a religion of nationalism which makes each State an end in itself, an end to which truth and morality, justice and civilization are of necessity subordinated. The Church is in bondage to the State. In the last War the pacifists, with the exception of the Quakers, were outside the official churches. Jesus protested against uniting the gospel to a Jewish nationalism. The Anglican Church is linked up with British Imperialism even as the Greek Church in Russia was bound up with Czardom. The national Churches of Christianity constitute an open revolt against the gospel of Jesus. The teaching of Jesus as professed by the West has not been assimilated by the people. The dignitaries of the Church are alarmed if any of its followers take the gospel of Jesus seriously and put it into practice, though they are quite willing to use Jesus as a decorative symbol in stained glass windows of dimly lit churches.

Emerson observed that every Stoic was a Stoic, but it is difficult to find Christians in Christendom. Nietzsche remarked that there was only one Christian in the world and he died on the Cross.

X

RELIGION AND THEOLOGY

While the course of religion ran from East to West, the course of theology ran in an opposite direction. The intellectual religion of the West with its love of law, order and definition has its striking virtues as well as its defects, even as the intuitive religion of the East has. The one brings to the common stock prudence, knowledge and discipline; the other freedom, originality and courage. The meeting of the two to-day may pave the way for a firm spiritual unity, if mutual appreciation takes the place of cold criticism and patronizing judgment. In the East the exaggerated respect for spiritual life has issued in an indifference to those material conditions in which alone the spiritual intention can be carried out. The Eastern spirituality became petrified in dead forms which are effete and corrupting. Our conservative pandits seem to approach the problem with the mind of the schoolmen, dealing with words and texts rather than with facts and truths. Our radicals, whose minds are barren of initiative and are untouched by vital experience, revel in second-hand imitations of the West. The superiority of Western religion lies in the fact that the individual seeks his salvation in service to others. It is not enough to retire into solitude to seek closer contact with the divine. Religion is not only life-transcending but also life-transforming. True worship is in the service of suffering humanity. Religion *qua* religion affirms the startling doctrine of the immeasurable value of every human soul. The ecstasy of a conscious equality of all souls melts the barriers between man and man. True religion with its intuition of the unity of the human race works for a spiritual community. It dare not stop at nations and continents but must embrace the whole human race. This very love of man requires us to appreciate other peoples' beliefs, a feature in which the Eastern faiths are superior to the Western. It is a common human desire to enforce our own ideas and standards on our fellow men. We all have a sort of sneaking sympathy with this frame of mind. There is nothing more detestable than contempt for honest opinion, especially when that opinion is attached to the spiritual yearnings of mankind. To-day we are not slaves to words as we were. We are able to see the life behind the labels. The time may come sooner than many of us expect when churches, temples and mosques will welcome all men of good will, when faith in God and love of man will be the only requisites for mutual fellowship and service, when the whole of humanity will be bound by one spirit though not by one name. Walter Pater in his book on *The Renaissance* tells the story that when the ship-load of sacred earth from the soil of Jerusalem mingled with the common clay of the Campo Santo at Pisa, a new flower grew up from it unlike any that man had seen before—a flower of rarely blended colours and rich complexity of tissues. May it not be that there will flourish through the ages to come, from the mixture and handling of the Eastern and the Western religions, such a flower of exquisite beauty and profusion?

LECTURE III

CHAOS AND CREATION

CHAOS AND CREATION[1]

"AND the earth was without form and void; and darkness was upon the face of the deep. And the spirit of God moved upon the face of the waters."[2] The Book of Genesis has received much adverse criticism, and its account of creation has been subjected to a severe scrutiny from the scientific standpoint. Christian preachers have found in it a perpetual theme for their Sunday addresses, and it will be a difficult time for those in my position if once the controversy between science and religion is set at rest.

I

SCIENCE AND RELIGION

I am not concerned to-day with the exposition of the account of creation given in Genesis as a historical fact or as a literal truth. Religion is not science, and if it trespasses into the region of the latter it does so at its own risk. When a Bishop Lightfoot writing in 1618 declared that man was created by the Trinity about 4004 B.C., and about nine o'clock in the morning, he was poaching upon the preserves of descriptive science and was only

[1] Sermon delivered at Manchester College, Oxford, November 1929.   [2] Genesis i. 2.

inviting criticism. For such a statement concerns the mechanism of the world, which is a problem for science, and not its mystery, which is the subject of religion.

The scientific interpretation of the universe which resolves the world into an invisible game of billiards, where the atoms are the balls which collide and pass on their motion from one to another, states only how things happen and not why. Even in those who think that further questions are unnecessary, there stirs the awareness of an attitude as yet unrealized. They vaguely feel that the universe has a depth of being beyond that made known to the senses or the intellect. Our sense of wonder and our sensitiveness to the environing mystery are in no way diminished by progress in science. We blush with shame if we remember our conceit in thinking that we are the centre of the world and the fairest work of God, while we are only temporary dwellers in the planetary system of a second-rate star many times smaller than countless others.

Those who are familiar with the cosmological speculations of the higher religions are aware that there are some common traditions which these religions employ. The traditions are plastic and there is more in them than meets the eye. They are the vehicles for spiritual ideas, and if we use them to-day it is because of the spiritual significance which they convey. Our text symbolizes, among other things, the insufficiency of the universe and its dependence on a supreme spirit transcending it. That the universe is not self-sufficing, that it is a deep unfathomable mystery, that it calls for explanation and that the explanation can only be in terms of a supreme intelligence and purpose, all these are assumed in the account. "Who is it that sends the rain? Who is it that thunders?" old Strepsiades asks of Socrates in *The Clouds* of Aristophanes; and the philosopher replies, "Not Zeus but the Clouds." "But," questions Strepsiades, "who but Zeus makes the clouds sweep along?" to which Socrates answers: "Not a bit of it; it is atmospheric whirligig." "Whirligig," muses Strepsiades, "I never thought of that—that Zeus is gone and that Son Whirligig rules now in his stead"; and so the old man satisfies himself by attributing consciousness to the whirlwind. In exchanging Zeus for a whirlwind, God for matter or *élan vital*, we also do the same thing. Modern Science is not opposed to the wisdom of the old words: *In the beginning, God.* One of the leading scientists, Sir James Jeans, tells us that the universe to the astronomer looks to be more a great thought than a great machine, and its author is more a mathematician than a mechanic. At the back of things we discern a great mind.

II

WITHOUT FORM AND VOID

"And the earth was without form and void; and darkness was upon the face of the deep." The Vedic

hymn of creation uses the same metaphor of waters
—*apraketam salilam sarvam*. The original condition
was one of chaos, of confusion and disorder, of
anarchy and unsettlement with which the mind is
not satisfied. It is one of utter darkness. The stars
are not shining.

"The spirit of God moved on the face of the
waters." The other version says it "brooded" on
the waters.[1] The spirit of God brooded over the
waste and the void, and brought forth light and
life. This symbol of brooding is taken from the
traditional cosmogony, where the world is com-
pared to an egg and God is figured as a bird brooding over it. The brooding power of a birdlike deity
is responsible for the production of life and light.
In the Upaniṣads also we have the metaphor of
God brooding over the world egg.[2] Only brooding
is not taken literally. Tapas, the energizing of conscious force, austere thinking, the inward travail
of the spirit, is the "brooding" which is responsible
for the creative work. Tapas is the force by which
some mighty possibility is actualized. *Sa tapo tapyata
sa tapas taptva idam sarvam asṛjata*. "He performed
tapas; having performed tapas he produced all this
whatsoever."[3] Tapas here means austere thinking
or reflection.[4] The ordered world is wholly the pro-

[1] *Genesis*: Cambridge Bible for schools and colleges.
[2] *Aitreya Upaniṣad*, i. 4; iii. 2.
[3] *Taittiriya Upaniṣad*, ii. 6. 1.; *Bṛhadāraṇyaka Upaniṣad*, i. 2. 6.
[4] Cf. Yasya jñānamayam tapah. "Whose tapas is in essence
jñāna." *Muṇḍaka Upaniṣad*, i. 1. 9.

duct of brooding, of intelligent and purposive activity. The successive acts of creation detailed in the first chapter of *Genesis* are due to this power of the spirit which creates world after world in order to realize itself. By brooding on inner states we let them take outward shape. We help life to utterance. This creative activity will continue until spirit has gained the final victory.

We move on from the beginning of creation to our own time. In the beginning, says the Bible, was the void; we have it still. To use the words of Jeremiah, "when the fruitful place was a wilderness and all the cities thereof were broken down," it is a state of chaos (iv. 26). The world is a chaos to-day. The amount of production has increased enormously, and though it is enough to feed and clothe the teeming population of the world, there is excessive poverty. We live miserable lives in a world of enormous wealth. While the economic facts like the war debts, the present depression and the increasing mechanization establish beyond doubt the interdependence of States, we are building up tariff walls and customs barriers and increasing national rivalries. Medical art has attained a high level of efficiency, and it is possible for us to live more easily and comfortably; and yet we do not live healthy and wholesome lives. The political situation is utterly distracting; for a world of independent nation States is little adapted to the present state of civilized humanity. The foundations of society are crumbling. The ancient virtues are flouted as outworn. Our social conventions are declared to be mere fictions and we no longer observe them. We have a good deal of penury, suffering and worry with us. The great achievement of power seems to have turned to distress and danger in our hands. It may not be physical pain and hunger, but there is a deeper suffering, a more poignant sickness of soul. Our world is a nude one which has torn off its old clothes and has failed to procure new ones. Faced by this disorder and confusion, we seem to be simply drifting, led by those who trade upon old traditions. No amount of skilful phrasing, no manipulation of old formulas can help us to restore meaning to life.

III

MAN THE CREATOR

How are we to get rid of the void and the waste, the chaos and the darkness? The text tells us that we should invoke the spirit which brooded over chaos, the spirit of truth, the spirit of love. Man is made in the likeness of God, in His own image. The vast cosmic impulse has embodied itself in him. He is an active and purposeful force in the world. His duty is not to mark time and wait on chance. As Blake's prophet said, when he beheld Albion on the precipice, "Why stand we here trembling around calling on God for help, and not ourselves in whom God dwells?" Man is himself a creator along with God. The scheme of the world is one of co-operative creation. Spirit and the waters, creator and creation, represent one single total situation which is changing every moment; and the quality of the growth depends on the quality of the spirit brought to bear on it. God insists on the creative activity of man. It alone changes the world and makes history. We must shoulder our share of creative responsibility. "Ah, Love, could you and I with Him conspire." It is the open conspiracy with God to which we are called. By creating us, God has invited us to the task. We cannot abandon civilization to chance. We must identify ourselves with the spirit of God moving on the face of the waters, enter into the very spirit of the universe and become its vehicles.

IV

BROODING, SUFFERING, THINKING

We are all interested in building order out of chaos, in getting things straightened. For it we require brooding, which is not suffering for its own sake. We need not make a cult of suffering. Millions suffered in the last war. Nine millions lost their lives. Many more abstained from alcohol and sugar, but to what end? Was that waste worth while? Was that abstinence purposeful? Did it help to bring about a better international situation? We need not go out of our way to incur needless hardship or seek martyrdom. If it is possible to do the right easily and happily, it should be done. Only we should not shirk doing the right simply because we cannot do it with ease and comfort. Brooding is not to be confused with suffering for its own sake, though it involves, as we shall see, an element of suffering.

Nor is brooding mere thinking, though it is thinking. The calm of vision should precede the tumult of creation. We must know what the facts are, and have an idea of what things ought to be. "In the beginning was the word." This ought to mean: "In the beginning was the Idea." The word is the expression of the idea. All creation is realization of an idea. Shah Jahan had the dream of the Taj in his mind before it became a structure at Agra. "Our minds build cathedrals before the workmen have moved a stone; and our minds destroy them before the elements have worn down their arches," says Whitehead the philosopher. Order is a vision in the soul before it is an accomplished fact in history. It is essential to all creation that we should form right ideas. We do not copy what is given, nor repeat what is old. We see beyond the "is"; we think beyond what is presented to us. There is the invisible pattern in our lives which makes us dissatisfied with the finite and the finished that confronts us.

But mere thinking will not carry us far. Schopenhauer says that "The wise men of all times have always said the same, and the fools, that is the immense majority, of all times have always done the same, that is to say, the opposite of what the wise have said; and that is why Voltaire tells us that we shall leave this world just as stupid and as bad as we found it when we came here." The world does not suffer so much from an insufficient knowledge of the truth as from an imperfect control of mind which makes the pursuit of truth difficult. Human actions proceed on beliefs and convictions, and not ideas and thoughts. Not mere knowledge is power, but faith. Even untruths work when once we believe in them, though they cannot work long. The Bolshevists win because they have motive power, the faith, which in sufficient measure the reformers and the pacifists lack.

Brooding is thinking with one's whole mind and one's whole body. It is integral thinking. It is making one's whole organism, sense and sensibility, mind and understanding, thrill with the idea. There is no function or organ of the body which is beyond the influence of the mind or the soul. Man is one psyche, one whole, of which body, mind and spirit are aspects. Donne's magnificent lines about the blushing girl describe this oneness:[1]

> Her pure and eloquent blood
> Spoke in her cheeks, and so distinctly wrought
> That one might almost say her body thought.

[1] *An Anatomy of the World*, l. 244, Donne's poems: Bullen, vol. ii. p. 135.

It is no use mistaking man for a merely intellectual being. His intellect is not his whole being. We must allow the idea framed by reason to sink into the subsoil of man's life and leaven the whole of his nature, conscious and unconscious. The word, the thought, must become flesh. Only such an alteration of the whole psychology of man, such a transformation of his whole being, such integral understanding, is creative in character. Creation is man's lonely attempt to know his own strange and secret soul and its real vocation.

V

KNOWING AND BEING

The discordant elements of mind and heart can be harmonized only in the solitude of the soul. There is all the difference in the world between those who believe in God with their intellects repeating the first article of the Creed, and those who believe in it with their whole being. The difference between us ordinary men and the saints is just here. It is a very hard thing to believe in God. It requires a hero to do so. The possession of the idea is not the same as the possession of the state or quality of mind. Ordinarily our intellectual concepts are divorced from our actual life. Our real motives are not our conscious ends. That we can become wise without effort, by listening to a sermon, by repeating a prayer, by reading a book is a most soothing dream; but it is only a dream. We must let the belief ripen and take possession of us by means of steady contemplation. It is an intimate and compelling process very like natural process, by which the mind that holds an idea becomes held by it.

Again, love of neighbour is with many of us an article of belief, but with the saints it is a part of their being. It is easier to repeat all that is said about love than to love one's fellows and have satisfactory relations with them. Love requires the searching eye of imagination, and one cannot lend imagination to those who have it not. Love is that imaginative consciousness which one has to develop in the loneliness of the soul, a consciousness which suffers and finds intolerable the suffering of another. If we are destitute of that mode of consciousness, we are not really human. True love regards the whole world as one's country and all mankind as one's countrymen. Such a love is a distant ideal. For we do not love the coloured man as a neighbour to the extent that we set him free from the state of servitude. We do not love the poor man's daughter enough to protect her from a fate which we shudder to think of as falling on one of our own. Love means renunciation of one's own self, of one's own standards. It is seeing with the other man's eyes, feeling with his heart and understanding with his mind.

I may relate here one of the numberless stories in Buddhist literature. A young lady, a healthy child of nature full of animal spirits, met Upagupta, the

disciple of Buddha, one fine evening and made
advances to him. He was in a dialectical mood.
She checked him and said: "Do not talk to me
about stars and saints, the suffering of the world
and the plan of the cosmos. They are not in my
line. I believe in warm, natural, happy, healthy
life. What the blood feels and believes is all that is
real for me." With difficulty Upagupta got out of
the situation that evening, not before promising to
return on another occasion. Long years elapsed.
The young lady of leisure and life, of wealth and
beauty, with her easy morals, made a mess of them
all till she decayed and became a mass of rotting
flesh, festering with sores, stinking with horrible
odour. As if this were not enough, she committed
a crime for which she was condemned to have her
limbs cut off. Despised and rejected by all, she
was turned out of the city gates and left on the spot
where her punishment was carried out. A few years
ago she was a spirit aflame with zeal, now nothing
but a mass of weakness and helplessness. No more
revolt, no more passion, not even complete darkness,
just emptiness. Accepting nothing, refusing to be
touched, to be questioned, to be cared for, remain-
ing empty, she saw through everything. No one
can deceive her again. In what she thought her last
moments, amid prayers and silent weeping, she
remembered her interview with Upagupta and felt
a gentle touch. Her eyes found Upagupta shining
with an unearthly radiance and vitality, looking

down on her, tender with a mother's love for a sick child. He noticed in her eyes an expression of anxiety, distress and self-reproach, an appeal for mercy. She said: "Upagupta, when my body was adorned with brilliant jewels and costly clothes and was as sweet as a lotus flower, I waited for you in vain. While I inspired flaming desire, you came not. Why come you now to witness this bleeding and mutilated flesh full of horror and disgust?" Upagupta gently stroked her hair, stirred her whole being and said, "Sister, for him who sees and understands, you have lost nothing. Do not regret. I love you, believe me. Do not covet the shadows of the joys and pleasures which have escaped you. My love to you is deeper than what is based on vain appearances." Her eyes brightened, her lips parted and with a new sense of well-being and lightness of heart, she became his disciple, which is another illustration that saints start their careers by first losing their characters! It needs a great soul to respond to a soul in torment.

One should always have love and not mercilessly oppress even those who have caused us suffering. When we love, we have no right to despise, however low the loved one may have fallen. If we love, what the loved one does will remain just as lovable. Those who disown the poor and the unfortunate, who satirize the guilty, humiliate the criminal and sneer at failures are not the truly loving. By striking down the stricken and flattening the prostrate, they are only playing the pharisee. The genuine men are patient with the worst of us, respect us enough to forgive us everything, invent endless excuses for us and care for us not as a duty but out of natural love. Without remembering our meannesses and misdeeds, they give us freely of their love and do not expect any return or require any repayment. For they know that a careless act sometimes makes havoc of a life and a rash deed shadows a home with shame. If a generous nature is not available or attractive, the wounded souls can only shrivel and die.

VI

THE COST OF RELIGION

Most of us wish to pick up religion as easily as a shell from the sand. We have not the patience or the energy for the laborious quest. As we get books from Blackwell, eggs from the farmer or medicines from the chemist, we expect the parson or the priest to provide us with religion at the cost of a few shillings or an hour a week. But it costs a good deal to be religious. The translation of ideas and intentions into realities has not been easy since the beginning of human effort. There was nothing which Buddha the great prince of India lacked, a kingdom, a home and every conceivable happiness. He had to deny himself all these, reject them, not out of hardness of heart, but out of love for truth.

Only thus could he conquer his own impulsive nature and make of himself a mirror of the universe. The assumption of the sorrows of humanity, ascribed by Christianity to the condescension of a super-natural person, is imposed on every man by the mere fact of his being born into the world. Happy is he who recognizes and fulfils his duty, though it exacts a price, in toil, suffering and blood.

VII

THE FUTILITY OF MERE PACIFISM

We are prepared to-day to endure toil and suffering for climbing the highest mountains or planting the flag in the extremes of the world, though not for ideas we have set ourselves as worthy of pursuit. Many of us think that we are working for peace, though the will to peace is only a pious and remote aspiration, a dim and distant idea and not a burning conviction which we are prepared to maintain by our blood and life. The glory of patriotism is some-thing for which we are prepared to pay a heavy cost. We have not the same sense of urgency about peace and international understanding as we have about our prosperity. Our love of humanity is not strong enough to overcome our fanaticism for country. We have no scruples in wiping out masses of men for wagon loads of rubber or oil wells. It is a delusion to think that the nations are becoming too well educated and enlightened for wars. It is the sand in which we are burying our heads. It was observed in the last war that there was a better feeling among the masses of people than among the intellectuals. All this is because our thought is superficial. We do not think, because we are afraid that it may cost us dearly. It may upset our plans and schemes. We simply do what the other man does. The pull of the crowd is irresistible. In the Middle Ages the Church exercised a tyranny over the people; now the jingoes do it. A few demagogues and adventurers with their control over the press and the radio lay down the law, and the masses unthinkingly march to their death. Our wills, our minds are not our own. A machine stronger than ourselves has made tools of us all. We are dressed in uniforms which enter our flesh. The silence of steel suppresses our sense of values. We are unable to look facts in the face. Hatred is made so agreeable and dished up so attractively that we revel in it, though we have no knowledge of the thing we hate. We are called cowards if we do not hate enough to kill. What is called discipline substitutes the certainty of being killed if we do not go to the front for the chance of being killed if we go. We take the risk and gain credit for courage. We wish for the death of brothers in arms, and slay without hatred, like machines, men whom we do not know, against whom we have absolutely no cause of enmity. Held in the terrible vice of wartime discipline, which forbids one to think, we kill by command, not by conviction. We are brave enough to suffer, to accept sorrow, but not brave enough to reject suffering for the sake of superstition. We fight for our symbols, trade, property, empire, symbols which have become stale and petrified. We have not the courage to cast off the old symbols, the outworn traditions, which have become fetters. We cannot shake them off, because the process of false education starts in the nurseries. Tradition and romance and all the unconscious influences of education have been for centuries directed towards the glorification of the independent sovereign State and the suppression of others as the most direct expression of loyalty to one's own State.

The dazzling prizes which await those who rattle the sword, the glamour of war, its heroism and self-sacrifice, are still dangled before the eyes of poor humanity, by the glitter of badges and stars, the jingle of bayonets and medals, by triumphal arches and military displays. By training and tradition we are urged to hate others, a hate which consumes both ourselves and our antagonists. The words of the second verse of the National anthem adopt the ethics of the tribal communities which we are supposed to have abandoned. When the demon of hatred takes possession of us, inflammable men and excitable women, we are stampeded like Gadarene swine into the deeps of war.

VIII

CHANGE OF MIND AS A WHOLE

To refuse to live up to the light within us is real sin; to refuse to live up to the ideas of the crowd around us is conventional sin. We are afraid of conventional sin and so commit real sin. The duty of man is to bear witness to the light within and if necessary to defy the conventions. The first need for peace is honest thinking. After all, man is a moral being and he will not generally undertake warfare unless it be justified on moral grounds. He professes creditable motives like making the world safe for democracy, protecting our hearths and homes, defending our women and children, upholding the integrity of treaties. The real motives of fear and pride, love of money and desire for power, are concealed. From the beginning, it is men's stupidity rather than their wickedness that is responsible for much of human suffering. Witches were tortured because we were required to save them from the clutches of the devil. Heretics were burnt because that seemed the only way to save them from eternity of burning in hell. We follow those who organize slaughter on a large scale because we are persuaded that that is the way to safeguard justice and liberty. Our worst cruelties seem to be expressions of our generosity.

Success in war does not mean victory for the right. It is a delusion to think that the only method

of showing that we are in the right is to destroy as
many of the other side as we possibly can. We must
realize the horrors of war, that it is essentially a
bestial thing, a surrender of all humanity, culture
and values. Its heroisms are its by-products. War
under modern conditions is not only wrong but
criminal. Now that bayonets and rifles have yielded
to chemicals, destruction will be universal, and no
distinction can be made between combatants and
non-combatants, men, women and children.

Pacifism is not a thing to be purchased from the
League of Nations. The moral inertia of mankind
requires to be overcome. The ability to resist the
tyranny of the masses is not easily acquired.[1] We
must convert the pacifist creed into a conviction
and possess the courage and the temper to live in
accordance with it. In other words, our whole consciousness, not merely the intellect, must be pressed
into service. We must will peace with our whole
body and mind, our feelings and instincts, our flesh
and its affections. An intellectual allegiance to paci-

[1] On February 9, 1933, the Oxford University Union after
a full debate in a large house carried the motion, "That this
house will in no circumstances fight for its king and country,"
by 275 votes against 153. The President of the Union, writing
in the *New Statesman and the Nation* (February 18, 1933), points
out that the Union decided that "the best method of ending
war was that of individual resistance to any future war."
The University Unions of Manchester, Cardiff and Glasgow
arrived at the same conclusion. All those gentlemen who
condemn war in theory and support it in practice were outraged at the crude courage of the University students.

fism is powerless against the unconscious impulses which hold our consciousness in thrall. The division between our inherited habits and institutions and our individual views and sentiments is profound. Our conscious desires contradict the deeply rooted instincts and so do not express our true personality. Our intellect might find war repellent and even inconsistent with humanity, but our whole nature must disapprove of it, to the extent that we are ready to suffer pain and loneliness rather than outrage our nature. This means not only changing our view but reorganizing our emotions. We must begin to think of the world not in terms of maps and markets but of men and women. We must not avoid the labour of imagination to understand the other man's point of view, look at things with the other man's eyes, even if we are not prepared to share his feelings. A character in one of Galsworthy's plays says:—if there was only one prayer for me to make, it would be this: "O Lord, give me the power to understand." The other races and the other peoples, however backward they may be, have also a place in the sun, a context in eternity. They are all fellow pilgrims on the onward journey, who are making the best of their circumstances. Each of us is a trustee for the health and happiness of humanity. We cannot exaggerate the magnitude of this trust, and it imposes on us the obligation to bear with each other's foibles, help each other over the obstacles and build the peace of the world.

IX

YOGA

There is an Indian saying that words are the daughters of earth but deeds are the sons of heaven. Words are born of intellect, deeds of spirit. It is faith that can move mountains. Faith is an attitude of will, the energy of soul, the response of the entire self. In faith we believe not only with our brains but with our whole soul and body. The idea is not merely thought out but grows from the deepest layers of life and mind. Not without reason do the Hindus equate jñāna with inward realization. The ideas we play with are simple affectations, rootless and sapless, and if they are to become creative they must become rooted in life. We must allow the ideals, the plans and the suggestions that flit before us to possess us, dominate us, transform us, recreate us. We must let ourselves be gripped and shaped by them until we become living images of them. Most of the time we are never in contact with things, but only with the words that stand for them. We make them vital by communing with them, by brooding over them. Only brooding or communion is truly generative. We can recreate the world only by self-creation, by profound personal transformation.

It is not a question of talking all the time but listening also, not of praying but of waiting in patience. "I open my mouth and pant for thy commandment" says the Psalmist. The command-

ment can be heard only if we sink from the surface
into the depths of our being and learn from the
fullness of life. The system of Yoga asks us to resort
to quietness and meditation. Pascal is right when
he says that "most of the mischief in the world
would never happen, if men would only be content
to sit still in their parlours." Even worship is a
means to gain solitude. But sitting still, being alone,
has become very difficult in these days. We devise
ways to escape from solitude, such as play and
drink, luxury and dissipation.

It is not enough to practise Yoga as many do
to-day in India and Europe, as a form of sport or
as a means of strengthening normal life-processes,
or for overcoming death or acquiring magical
powers. Self-unification, which is, as it were, an
inner rebirth, is the aim of Yoga. Its object is the
integration of the self, the spiritualizing of the non-
spiritual, the synthesizing of the multiple factors
which are inclined to assume autonomous *rôles*.
No decent house can be built if the foundations
are unsound. If the foundations are strong and the
base is deeply and solidly laid, the walls and the
pillars can be built up. From the things that happen
we must choose the idea appropriate to our consciousness and give ourselves up entirely to the new
way. Every man is an artist in life; he creates his
own life-pattern with reference to the material at
his disposal. We cannot force it into another shape.
There is an immanent form or ideal, the *daimon* in

us which has to be discovered and developed. When the psychoanalyst asks us to trace out our forgotten memories, our unknown desires, and acquire a knowledge of the hidden forces at work in ourselves and adapt ourselves to the demands of reality, he is asking us to awaken our true nature and transform all our impulses into the means of its expression. So long as one does not realize one's immanent nature one is not entirely oneself. Each of us is like a stringed instrument which will not yield its proper music until the tension of the strings is just. Each of us must discover his proper tension by continual exploration and adjustment. Yoga aims at the discovery of self and the transformation of the totality. The first demand of Yoga is that all life should become a meaningful whole and every element of life should be inspired by the spirit.

Gestalt psychology regards the human mind as a totality; but a totality is not necessarily a system or a harmony, since it may contain within it discordant elements, conflicting impulses, inner tensions. Yet insistence on totality reveals how every occurrence, every experience is a function of the whole and changes to some extent the nature of the whole. Two persons, who undergo the same experience, may react to it in different ways because the two totalities are different. The self is a dynamic whole, a historical movement, with the result that the same experience does not possess the same significance at different periods of life. A totality is not a collection or a sum of the different elements, but a whole with meaning and coherence. In other words, the elements of the totality are chaotic and formless and require to be informed, to be given a significance, a soul as it were, which combines the different elements, in themselves meaningless, into a satisfactory pattern even as sounds are combined to form a melody. Then life becomes intense and ordered and revolves with immense energy about a steady centre exhibiting rhythm and harmony. Any upsetting of this balance means broken rhythm and disharmony.

One of the most frequent causes of failure in life, of mental and physical breakdown, is what the psychologists call conflict. There is an opposition between our conscious duty and our inclination, buried deep in the unconscious, which shows itself in certain morbid sentiments. Freud's great contribution to mental therapy is in his view that much of the unhappiness in the world is traceable to unconscious conflict, which can be overcome by realizing and resolving the conflict. When the personality is divided or distracted, there can be no effective work or happiness. There is the need for the single eye within, the closest correspondence between the secret thoughts and the overt desires. We cannot find out easily our secret impulses or deep desires. We cannot find ourselves, unless we use our leisure and solitude in contemplation. However difficult it may be, it is still the appointed way. Religion does not consist so much in prayers and rites as in those silent hours of self-communion which will help us to control our character and build up our personality. By it we cleanse our thoughts, purify our emotions and let the seed of spirit grow. The art of letting things grow in quietness, action in non-action, as the Bhagavadgītā has it, is Yoga. It is the growth of the soul, without any interference from conscious thinking. This growth is the natural thing, our normal destiny, and yet is the most difficult of all things, because our consciousness is for ever interfering, correcting, hindering the simple growth of the psyche. It requires steady pursuit of the end. "Wisdom is not to be won," said Plato, "unless a man make himself a slave to its winning." We must concentrate or hold on to the idea, blot out everything else and use all our resources for fixing it in the mind. We can write it down, visualize it, paint or draw or model figures until it sinks into the unconscious and recreates us. The very sincerity of our effort will carry us forward, until we reach the goal of a synthesis of the conscious and the unconscious, when our whole being is filled with one idea and our life acquires a meaning and a content. The peculiar sensitiveness of the soul to its special destiny proceeds from a slow cleansing of its life by penetrating prayer, deep reflection and contact with genuine men. When the soul realizes its vocation, its being is perfected by the force of life itself. It shall no more wander helplessly on the surface of life; but having found its direction, it lives for the eternal values in the midst of time.

X

TAPO BRAHMA

What is true of the individual is true of the community. The fundamental cause of the discords of the world, the chaos of thought in politics, the confusion of standards in ethics is due to intellectual specialization at the expense of the cultivation of the whole man. We are unable to relate the particular fragments of truth to the infinite truth, which, though not seen with the eyes of intellect, is still so vital for us that we are prepared to fight for it and be crushed to the earth for its sake. The warring impulses of our social life require to be reconciled if we are not to wander through a world without meaning. Philosophy and religion help us more than the exact sciences in discovering a goal for human conduct, a unity for the higher endeavours of the human mind.

Brooding, not reasoning, meditation, not petition, results in an enlargement, an elevation, a transformation of one's being and thus a recreation of the world. By closing our eyes and looking within, by contemplation or brooding, we change our inner nature. Heaven is lost or found in the inner self. We brood and build. We energize and create. God brooded on the waters and brought forth life. Brooding is creative energy. Tapo Brahma.

LECTURE IV

REVOLUTION THROUGH SUFFERING

REVOLUTION THROUGH SUFFERING

I

RELIGION AND OTHERWORLDLINESS

THE text I propose to consider is the 26th verse of the Twenty-first Chapter of Ezekiel. "I will overturn, overturn, overturn it; and it shall be no more until he come whose right it is and I will give it him."

Religion, it is said, proclaims an ethic of submission and quietism. It is a matter between God and one's own soul, and has little to do with the world. It exalts the ascetic who flees from the world in order that he may live quite alone with his God. We seek to gain the life eternal by renouncing the temporal. An Arab thinker said: "This world and the other are like the two wives of one husband—if he pleases one, he makes the other envious." Such a view of the tragic conflict between God and the world gives point to the accusation brought against religion that it is a sort of opiate used to keep us indifferent to the woes of this world. Religion is said to be a convenient device invented by the well-to-do to keep the poor in poverty, the illiterate in ignorance, the sinful in degradation and the masses content with their servility. The Socialist thinkers from Marx downwards argue that their main motive is this-worldly.

[1] Sermon delivered at Manchester College Chapel, Oxford, 8, vi. 1930.

II

HEGEL AND MARX

In support of the view that religious philosophy implies a quietistic view of life, Hegel's authority is cited. For Hegel, logic "is the exposition of God as He is in His eternal essence before the creation of the world and man."[1] It is a development of ideas in terms of a timeless order of necessity and not in those of empirical succession. Hegel deduces the historical succession of things in time from the immanent development of ideas out of time. The world process is, for him, the method by which the cosmic subject attains to self-consciousness. Temporal existents are turned into ontological pre-existents. History is the autobiography of God, the march of the spirit towards freedom. The contingent world in space and time is a mere appearance. Such a doctrine seems to Marx to sanctify the existing order. Hegel's ambiguous formulas about the identity of the real and the rational do not clarify the situation. Hegel's philosophy does not seem to provide a sufficient motive for reforming or remaking existence. Advocates of social revolution find in Hegel a champion of social accommodation and political opportunism.

Such a view is not quite fair to Hegel, since for him everything finite, everything short of the absolute, is neither perfectly real nor perfectly reasonable. Since the existent is not synonymous

[1] *Science of Logic*, E.T., vol. i. p. 60.

with the real, Hegel's philosophy cannot be regarded as offering a justification for the *status quo*. The truly real is the perfectly ideal, not what is, but what ought to be. There is no finality about the established order. And yet there is point in Marx's criticism. If all finite existents are non-real, it is not easy to distinguish between the greater or lesser reality of any finite existence; between, say, a republican democracy and a communist oligarchy. Marx rightly accepts from Hegel the idea of history as a logical evolution. Only he turned Hegel's idea upside down. While for Hegel spirit (including art, morality and religion) is the determining factor of the economic system, for Marx, the economic system which has its own peculiar but irreversible dialectic is the causal factor from which the spiritual elements follow. There is more scope for the initiative of human individuals in Hegel's scheme. History is made by men. It is not the outcome of the automatic operation of impersonal forces, matter or spirit; it is the action of men in pursuit of definite ends. Human desires and purposes are the forces behind history. When Lenin speaks of the "will of history," of the inevitability of social upheavals, he is stressing one aspect of history. In a real sense, it is given to human individuals to influence and change the direction of events. Hegel, however, is more true to history when he asserts that ideas rule the material. Reason and will are imposed on economic factors and are not conditioned by them.

III

RELIGION AND SOCIAL REVOLUTION

True religion, however, agrees with the social idealists in affirming that life eternal is to be realized on this earth itself. Love of man is as fundamental to religion as worship of God. We must seek our evolution through the medium of this life, by transforming it, by changing it over. Social idealists believe in the discord between the ideal and the actual, the strife between two antagonistic world-orders, which is the essence of all religion. Faced by the sorrow and the suffering of the world, Buddha endeavoured to banish them. He did not ignore or explain them away, but as a profound revolutionary tried to overcome them. Jesus felt that the kingdom of heaven is ranged against the kingdom of this world. For St. Paul, the forces of this world are arrayed against those of the spirit. For Augustine the earthly power is fighting against the City of God. Religion is a challenge to replace the world of power by that of spirit. It is a summons to man to adventure and experiment.

God is a supreme revolutionary. He is not only the master builder but the master destroyer. Creation and destruction are correlative attributes of the deity. "Stepping over corpses," Hegel teaches us, "is the way in which the objective spirit walks in order to reach fulfilment." If a new and better order is to arise, the old order must be broken up. For genuine growth, life and space are necessary, and what is congesting the ground must be destroyed. We are surrounded by traditions that once were living but are now dead, not only in the spiritual world but in the political, social and industrial. Mere palliatives will not do; a radical change over, a complete overturning, is what is needed. Many intellectual, moral and physical upturnings of the soil are necessary to work out a little result. What we call anarchy, revolt, revolution, are the means by which progress is achieved.

All improvements are effected by the discontented, the agitators, the rebels, the revolutionaries, who are at war with the world of shams. They start new movements, expound new theologies, found new constitutions. Jesus rebelled against the pretensions of the priests, the pagan traditions of Imperial Rome and the conventional "good form" of his time. The social passion which animates and inspires the great heroes is not inconsistent with the fervour of religion; nay, it is its natural outcome. The saints of religion, the prophets whose souls are kindled by the sight of oppression and injustice are the men who have made the deepest impression on the organic substance of humanity. The practical rejection of religion with which Marxism is now identified seems to be needless. Simply because our interests are social, it does not follow that we should cut ourselves off from the spiritual. Spiritual awareness and social efficiency are not only consistent but also complementary. To ignore the spiritual is to restrict one's capacity for effective social work. The world is broken to pieces again and again until it is brought steadily nearer and nearer to perfection. So long as humanity is vile, crude and hard, there is no other way to smelt and shape it. The believers in God possess the faith that rebels. God is with the fence-breakers, the fermenters, the revolutionaries. His servants do not bring peace but dissension, for they steer by stars which the world cannot see; and therefore they are hated by it.

Will it do if we have in us the will to destroy? Is rebellion as such to be encouraged? We have to-day many cheap and easy revolts of the comfort-loving against spiritual restraints. Destruction is easy and attractive to violent tempers.

Are we to rebel for the sake of rebellion or has it any higher end? The text says, there is an end before it. There is such a thing as a final goal of evolution. Things are settled only when they are settled right. The world must be given to those whose right it is.

To whom does the world belong by right? Does it belong to those hard-headed, efficient, matter-of-fact commercial-minded men who possess it? Christian scriptures, like all other religious scriptures, declare "The Earth is the Lord's and the fulness thereof." *Īśāvāsyam idam sarvam*—"All this is pervaded by the Lord." If we are the servants of God, we must work for truth, for the truth which means the establishment of right relationships between man and man, community and community, nation and nation.

IV

LOVE AND SUFFERING

The meek shall inherit the earth. The meek are not the comfortable and the complacent, not the salaried parsons and priests who shrink from truth for fear of offending the crowds. We saw how in the last war the official exponents of every creed supported the warlike policies of their States. The pacifists, who were damned as atheists, were the meek, the persecuted; they stood against the war and faced the worst that men did. The text says that the world will be taken away from the proud and the efficient and given over to the meek and the suffering. "I shall exalt him that is low and abase him that is high." The worldly standards require to be overturned. Even at the moment when Jesus was absorbed by His work, His followers were discussing who among them was to be the greatest. When the shadow of the Cross was darkening the horizon, they were obsessed by the thought of place and power. If a man is to be great, he must be content to become of no account; and if he would be chief, it must be by pre-eminence in service and sacrifice. To-day we are filled with the same worldly ideas of power and pre-eminence. Gentleness is not necessarily a quality of a gentleman. It is treated as a feminine virtue. The obligation of the strong to help the weak is the basis of all civilized life. But we are taught in our homes and schools that the strong have the right to the service of the weak. This amazing doctrine is the principle underlying our practice. Women being the weaker sex should be bondslaves of the male. Backward nations, by which is meant physically weaker ones, should be content to wait on the stronger powers. But religion proclaims the opposite truth that the strong should wait on the weak. To whom much is given, of the same shall much be required. If we pride ourselves on being the advanced nations, it carries with it an obligation for duty and service.

The world belongs to the leadership of love and service. The master is the servant. He who helps others willingly and effectively is the greatest of all. The pioneers, the reformers, are always the sufferers. Caught by a purpose greater than their own, they cannot turn back until the goal is reached. "In the world ye shall have tribulation." The religious view has nothing in common with the popular belief in happiness as the chief aim in life. Even when philosophers adopt the hedonistic view of pleasure as the chief good, they mean by pleasure spiritual happiness and not material comfort or physical satisfaction. They hold up suffering as the chief means to perfection or spiritual happiness. It is the power of love and sacrifice that can refashion the world which is chained to-day in fetters of hatred and suspicion. In proportion as men try to be self-sufficient and self-regarding, they become maimed and mutilated. They become whole and pure to the extent that they possess love.

Love and suffering go together. They are like the two eyes. Dante looked at the lovers wearing through all the ages the supremest crown of sorrow. No one who really loves can escape suffering. The more you love, the more you suffer. To love is not to be less sorrowful but to be less vile. Life is a series of conflicts. The best of us stand facing each other unable to understand. Man and woman, parent and child, face each other in mutual opposition. In our world which is so rapidly changing, so perplexed and so unsure of itself, with its roots torn away, with its ideals radically changed, with its trust in all that age and tradition have sanctified rudely shaken, children do not look up to the parents, and the parents are uneasy and anxious when they should be serene and mellow. Can we turn away simply because we do not understand? Not if we truly love. Can we overcome the conflict by force? We cannot suppress by force our inward longings and our unfulfilled cravings. For a repressed desire is a potential foe. If we beat down our opponent, he will wait in ambush and beat us down when next the chance arises. A reconciled foe becomes a good friend; a beaten antagonist is a sworn enemy. Though violence may suppress wrong, it will increase bitterness. Violent resistance increases the spirit of ill-will. If we cannot overcome opposition by love, what remains is only endurance. We must endure or escape. Either way, it is not different from suffering. The passions and the aspirations, the loneliness and the love, we cannot communicate to others. The others do not understand. They believe the passion to be mean, the feeling to be trite; and if we love, we have to bear it all in meekness. In such situations one must keep one's ideas to oneself. This does not mean betraying one's inner integrity. On the other hand, one is guarding it by silence, protecting it by one's endurance. After all, even the most powerful forces will find it hard to cope with the transparency of love, of love which suffers to the utmost.

We are called upon to return good for evil. Consider Buddha's words: "Not by hate is hate destroyed; by love alone is hate destroyed." "Ye monks, if robbers and murderers should sever your joints and ribs with a saw, he who fell into anger thereat would not be fulfilling my commands."[1] The Hindu leaders from the times of the Upaniṣads have asked us to be tolerant even with the intolerant, to be gentle with the violent and be detached from all things even when living among those who are attached to them. Such an ideal may not appeal to

[1] "Even as a mother watcheth o'er her child,
　　Her only child, as long as life doth last,
　　So let us, for all creatures, great or small,
　　Develop such a boundless heart and mind,
　　Ay, let us practise love for all the world,
　　Above, below, around and everywhere,
　　Uncramped, free from ill-will and enmity."
　　(*Sutta Nipāta*, verses 149–150, Mrs. Rhys Davids, E.T.)

the active races with their strong sense of life, but it can cure hidden wounds and soften personal sorrows. There is nothing nobler on the scene of space and time than where good men and true women, who renounce comforts, suffer as outcasts and walk the pavements of the world in want, scattering love, without talking about it or feeling good or wanting anybody to know.

V

GOD IS LOVE

God is the loving friend of all—*suhridam sarvabhūtānām*, as the Bhagavadgītā has it. If Jesus won for spirit the victory, it was not by force and greed, but by patient love and suffering. The great saying, "No one knows the Father except the Son," means that only one who loves deeply has an insight into the true nature of God as Father, whose character is suffering love. God is not the sovereign who exercises His divine rights and enforces His law, but is a tender, loving father who does not cease to love simply because we sin and fail. The essential truth of religion for which Jesus died on the Cross is stated thus by John in his Epistle: "Beloved, let us love one another, for love is of God. Every one that loveth is born of God and knoweth God. He that loveth not knoweth not God. For God is love." Not justice but love, spontaneous, uncalculating, is the deepest fact of the universe.

Love is not a passing sentiment or feeble emotion,

but an attitude of life involving mind, feeling and will, strong, deep and enduring. It has respect for the object loved, believes in its ultimate quality and seeks its highest good. We are members one of another, so that we cannot injure or help our neighbours without injuring or helping ourselves. It is not a question of whether there are or are not unlovable persons, but whether godliness does not mean loving persons even when they are not lovable. Wherever love rules life, life becomes a continuous act of giving without any desire for return. Its existence is inseparable from giving, though judged from without the latter may involve enjoyment or suffering. There cannot be any return for love which belongs to the spiritual plane. It can only be reciprocated or, more accurately, shared. It is purely disinterested, and cannot help being disinterested. Goethe's observation, "If I love thee, this is no concern of thine," insists on that quality of utter disinterestedness which is a component of true love, which lifts one who possesses it to the supernatural level. He who loves with such intensity becomes sacred.

VI

LOVE OF NEIGHBOUR

Love of neighbour which all religions profess means justice and respect for him and his individuality. To love one's neighbour is not to compel him to share our opinions, but to renounce one's own standards and see with the other man's eyes, feel with his heart and understand with his mind. It is not putting on a sour face when our neighbour follows the bent of his humour. It is to be open-minded and hospitable to the other's opinions. Turgeniev was commenting on love when he said, "it seems to me that to put oneself in the second place is the whole significance of life." "If meat makes my brother to offend, I will eat no flesh while the world standeth, lest I make my brother to offend."[1] If we are to be so particular even in matters of diet, how much more respectful should we be in matters of social life and religion? Every individual has the sacred right to live as he chooses. In our modern life we all wear the same kind of clothes, cut according to regulations; we obey the same social laws and our thoughts are moulded by the same traditions. We read the same papers, attend the same pictures and play the same games. We ape one another with such ridiculous slavishness, that our personalities are ignored. We have become worshippers of the god of decency.

It is sad to find that there are honest men and women even at this time of the day who believe that with them and them alone lies the truth, and anybody who does not share their opinions is sincerely to be pitied as if he were some unfortunate and inferior creature. It is an arrogant humility and

[1] 1 Cor. viii. 13.

spiritual haughtiness which shows itself in such excessive concern for the despised neighbour. True love demands that we recognize the individuality of our fellow-men and assist them to attain interior purity and integral union.

If we are spiritually alive, our capacity for love and service will be ever growing. We will be indulgent to others and hard on ourselves. The characteristic sign of a spiritual temper is to be inwardly hard and austere and outwardly genial and forgiving. Only the spiritual can rescue suffering souls and transfigure them. When we look back on our life, on those hours when we were surrounded by opportunities for understanding fellowship, we cannot escape the bitter regret that we did not make more of it when it was so near to us, that we were so blind and heartless and were not a little more tender, a little more kind. The memories which hurt us most when we stumble upon them are those of the occasions when we showed ourselves perverse and cold, when hungry eyes looked at us with wistful expectancy, when we warded off the loving impulse by some jealous sense of our own rights, some false pride of our own dignity, some craven fear of conventional good form, some petty notion of our own obligations, when we stifled the smile and withheld the hand and turned away in silence. Life is a series of lost opportunities. God presents us with chances, but it depends on us whether we embrace them or not.

VII

"JUDGE NOT"

When we come across the "guilty" and the "criminal," our modern world with its fixed standards upholds the good and punishes the guilty. To these exponents of flatness and sanity who seem to have developed a sixth sense for the detection of evil, good and evil are clearly defined and settled. Their dimensions and degrees are historically determined by the ancient sages and lawgivers. Our teachers have taught us the old rules and have accustomed us to them. The well-established code one has to follow blindly; if one does not, he must pay with his liberty, property, nay, life itself. If we pause and think we shall realize that the moral code is a convention and everything is hypothesis pure and simple, even such fundamental notions as time, space and cause. The world *knows* nothing, but assumes, takes for granted. Tradition and custom have in the past justified ever so many practices. We burnt widows, indulged in human sacrifices, enjoyed execution and torture, demanded hara-kiri; and we accepted them all as part of the recognized scheme of things. When any line of conduct is in conformity with social opinion, we feel that we are exempt from personal responsibility. To-day a State sacrifices millions of its citizens with a clean conscience in the name of war. Life has become one continuous ritual.

Belief in authority, however, depersonalizes the human being. We surrender our freedom of spirit when we accept another's judgment as final. A purely formal and phenomenal life is unworthy of a human being, though most of us lead such lives. All progress in human relations is due to the non-conformists who are unwilling to kill their imagination and starve their natural sympathy. Only those who are spiritually dead can worship good form and prefer it to a live heart and mind. The saints are offenders against good form, though the converse is not true. Only to the correct, life has no problems. While correctness is necessary for social security, it does not make for spiritual awareness.

When we recognize this fact, we shall be more cautious in condemning those who do not conform to custom. The guilt may be due to the force of circumstances, or to the impulse to express individuality. The youth who dies in his school days because his soul is shattered, the dazzling glowworms of girls who with their faked emotions make a young man's raw passions run high, how do we know that they do not have the divine in them? There is nothing in this world which is completely divine or hopelessly diabolic.[1] In all of us, in the small as well as in the great, in the humble as well as in the lofty, there is an instinct for beauty, a desire for truth, an infinite need for loving which make us divine. Even errors and weaknesses have a touching beauty of

[1] Dṛṣṭam kim api lokesmin na nirdoṣam na nirguṇam.

their own. People are found in abnormal circumstances. They commit crimes seized in a vortex of falsehood, in a world where normality is constantly replaced by conventionality, where simplicity and naturalness are crushed under a pile of lies, which are called laws. We fail to see that it is society that is abnormally arranged, and must be altered if we are to get rid of crimes and culprits. Besides, chance plays a large part in human life and it is the unlucky that are persecuted. They suffer and cry out in pain, and by punishing them we only wound them more deeply than ever.

There is only one who can say, "Vengeance is mine, I will repay." Human individuals must realize that they themselves are sinners and the only remedy open to them is love and mercy. There are no wicked beings, none but unfortunate creatures, and our only duty is to understand each other and love each other.

VIII

CREATIVE ART AND UNDERSTANDING

The function of art is to induce this mood of compassion. Not to idolize, not to condemn, but to humanize is its supreme task. The artist can do this only by looking into the secret impulses of the human soul and chronicling its dreams and aspirations. The great artist has that sense of deep community without which no real understanding is possible. He tries to live through a different history and experience it in imagination. When he succeeds in capturing the heart of life he can reveal the struggle and anguish of the soul, how it trembles at the brink of temptation and, seized with cold terror, is unable to say yea or nay. He lets his characters grow, flower and fade in their natural rhythm. He shows the vastness and variety of human life. Each individual becomes a determinate centre of the cosmic situation, with his own individuality. He breathes with his own breath, laughs with his own lips and weeps with his own tears. The contending forces are revealed; the souls are on the rack as it were, and we cannot help sympathizing with them. A great Sanskrit poet, Bhavabhūti, maintains that though the artist speaks of different moods of laughter, pity, compassion, anger, love, etc., they are all variations of a common theme, *Karuna*, compassion, love with suffering.[1]

A deep sense of the waste of good and torture of noble souls is the essence of all tragedy. Suffering takes us to the centre of things, and away from the trivialities of life. It reveals a sense of man's greatness, how much he could bear locked up in his heart. Serious souls enjoy plays which arouse pity and terror even as children and superficial persons do *Jack and the Beanstalk*. Falstaff does not attract us

---

[1] Eko rasah karuna eva nimittabhedād bhinnah prthakprthag ivāśrayate vivartān/ āvartabudbuda tarangamayān vikārān āmbo yathā salilam eva hi tat samastam//.

quite as much as Hamlet does, though both of them are equally garrulous. In the great domestic tragedies Shakespeare enlists our sympathy for the victims by holding up the mirror to life. The anguish and distraction of Hamlet are not un- expected. Claudius and Gertrude live adulterously, murder Hamlet's father, ascend the throne and deprive him of his succession. The sense of his mother's guilt preys on his mind. He turns to Ophelia, condemns her as a predestined adulteress though there is nothing to warrant it. He asks her to get to a nunnery, drives her mad and brings about her death. His will power is at its end. He is unable to reason logically and thoughts whirl through his brain. He looks at life and at death, and wonders which is worse. "To be or not to be." Macbeth goes through a bath of blood and ends with a commentary on life that it is an idle tale full of sound and fury but without any meaning. Othello kills his wife, kills himself and makes a complete hash of it all because a jealous villain worms himself into his confidence and plays on his weakness. Con- sider the condition in which men are seized by certain impulses which bind their movements, paralyse their powers of resistance and thought, and desire to struggle with the darkness that has fallen on their souls. The very stars in their courses seem to be fighting against them. They seem to be driven to their destruction. We find these terrible and yet acknowledge them to be sublime. Macbeth, Hamlet and Othello impress us not by their difference from us but by their likeness to us. There is perfect harmony between their action and their circumstances. Take Galsworthy's *Forsyte Saga*. The conflict of Soames and Irene, which underlies the whole story, reveals the struggle of human beings against fate quite as much as any tragedy of Aeschylus. Where sex attraction is utterly lacking in one partner, the repulsion implicit in nature cannot be overcome. The characters reveal themselves as it were in their predestined harmonies of suffering and joy. Only those destitute of imagination and real understanding will condemn them from the outside. We are impressed by the unity of life. It is one in all its myriad manifestations. Judge not, for it is all encompassed in the dark. There are no faults of which we ourselves might not have been guilty. The crimes of which the worst criminals are guilty are only overgrown expressions of weaknesses we all share. It is well to remind ourselves that we have no exact knowledge of the life and conditions of other human souls. We do not know another human being until the last secrets of the heart are revealed, and they may be secrets until the end of time. If only we could strip souls as easily as we strip bodies, we shall be less hard. There is a sense in which Socrates' saying that all wrongdoing is involuntary is true. Each of us has the desire for good, and if we do evil it is because we expect to gain good by it. Wrongdoing is due to miscalculation.

Behaviourism, which is becoming increasingly fashionable, holds that the inner life can be completely comprehended by the observer from outside. This view ignores the inner world of personal experience which is properly the sphere of the soul. How little do we know of our own! Can we explain our own situations to others, however utterly sincere we may be? The weaknesses of our own nature are tenderly hidden from us, and we deal with others armed with a breastplate of false pride and complacency.

Besides, have we not something to be grateful for even in the weaknesses of men? If we were surrounded by perfection and met only saints and heroes, we might fail altogether. It is when we find that the great of the world had their weaknesses like ourselves, their temptations, their hours of doubt and darkness, that we are inspired to effort. Their errors and sorrows comfort us. It is no dishonour to fail where they failed. Man grows from imperfection to perfection, through joy and sorrow, and the worst of us are made of the same clay as the best. There is a real kinship between great spirits and average men, and this is what increases the dignity and worth of human life.

Suffering is not punishment but the prize of fellowship. It is an essential accompaniment of all creative endeavour. To be unable to endure is moral weakness. We need not ask for pain, but it is a proof of strength to be able to face it. It is not for nothing that religions impose ardours and endurances. If religion asks us to renounce the good things of life for the sake of eternal values, it is because it believes that wrong can be righted and truth established by means of sacrifice deliberately undertaken. It assumes that suffering is something irremediable, and a noble soul must shake off that ultimate cowardice, the fear of death.

Suffering is not always a misfortune. It often helps us to grow. In the depths of sorrow we receive light. We improve through experiencing moments of weakness and hesitation. If we do not pass through dark and difficult moments of life, it is quite possible that we may grow hard and fall victims to pride and self-righteousness. It is when we are beaten by fate that we learn to bow our heads in silence and humility before the spirit of the universe. This idea is not by any means peculiar to the Hindus. It is suggested in the Proverbs[1] and is worked out in Ecclesiastes: "Accept whatsoever is brought upon thee, and be long suffering when thou passest into humiliation. For gold is tried in the fire and acceptable men in the furnace of affliction."[2] When we meet characters who have suffered, persons who have endured troubles of mind which are more serious than pains of the body, our pity for them has in it an element of reverence because they have come near in some way to the heart of truth. The men who will be of most worth to us are those who

[1] III. 11–12.

[2] II. 4–5.

faced difficulties and disappointments and not those whose hearts have not felt one real pang, whose lives have not known one crushing blow. All this does not mean that one should suffer for the sake of suffering. It is one's duty to remove all unhappiness, all avoidable suffering. By one's own suffering, if necessary, one should strive to remove life's abominations, its lies and sorrows.

IX

THE SPIRIT THAT REBELS

If we should wish to build a society in which judges and evildoers are transformed into higher beings, into brothers forgiving one another, and thus free themselves from falsehood, guilt and crime, we must practise love. The believer to-day is called upon to stand up against the old and the outworn and accept sorrow to lighten it. Only those who are devoid of the barren littleness of soul are prepared to bear the guilt of others. He who takes upon himself a nation's shame is the true leader. Suffering is the choice of the magnanimous. The soul of faith, though poor in body, finds a joy in facing the difficulties of life and overcoming them.

The mystery of life is creative sacrifice. It is the central idea of the Cross, which was such a scandal to the Jews and the Greeks, that he who truly loves us will have to suffer for us, even to the point of death. It is the truth central to all living religions.

The victory over evil through suffering and death, we have it not only in the garden of Gethsemane, in the palace of Gautama, the Buddha, in the cell where Socrates drank the hemlock, but in many other unknown places. Only that which suffers is truly loving, truly divine. Naturally men made a god of the Buddha who renounced the most precious human ties, of the Jesus who suffered and died; for they revealed the eternal essence of the living god who is Love. Blessed are those that suffer is the cry of all religions. Suffering is the substance of spiritual life, the very flesh of reality, the blood that unites us all. The Cross signifies that evil, in the hour of its supreme triumph, suffers its decisive defeat by the force of patient love and suffering. Those who follow the example of Jesus should prefer love to happiness, suffering to comfort. They should pray for the gift of love which means charity and compassion.

Religion tells us that the creative energy necessary for drastic reconstruction comes from communion with the eternal. Fellowship and service spring from spiritual sources. Altruism is not a substitute for adoration from which it arises.

In a sense we might say that the God who is responsible for this world, who is the consciousness of the universe, is working through brute matter from which He has to liberate Himself and liberate us. He Himself is suffering in each and all of us. This suffering will be at an end when the spirit which is imprisoned in transitory matter is released, when the potential world-spirit or spirit of the whole becomes the actual consciousness of each part, when God becomes (in the Apostle's words) "all in all," when the solitary limited God becomes the pantheistic God.

In the meantime the world belongs to the suffering rebels, the unarmed challengers of the mighty, the meek resisters who put truth above policy, humanity above country, love above force. The sacred compassion of youth for the dispossessed, for the slave selling his manhood or her womanhood for the prospect of a dole, his righteous indignation against those who neither toil nor spin and yet possess the abundance of possessions which they squander at will, are divine. Let us put heart into those rebels who fight for a finer art, a purer life, a cleaner race, unmasking imposture, overthrowing inequalities, replacing the false by the true. All religions proclaim with one voice, though in many languages, that we are summoned not to a light-hearted saunter or even to a journey where we can always walk with clasped hands of understanding and friendship, but to a battle where we have to fight the forces of stupidity and selfishness. Let us become soldiers on the march, soldiers of truth, soldiers fighting with love as our weapon, overturning the universe, until the reign of God is established on earth.

LECTURE V

RABINDRANATH TAGORE

RABINDRANATH TAGORE

LET me express at the outset my grateful appreciation of the kindness which the Organizing Committee have shown me by enabling me to participate in the events of this week and preside over the Conference to-day. While I regret that one more competent and familiar with the works of the Poet in the original Bengali is not in my place, I am grateful for this opportunity to pay my homage to his important work and profound influence on the country and the world at large.

I

THE GREATNESS OF LITERATURE

It is the peculiar glory of great literature that it lasts much longer than kings and dynasties. History bears witness to the power of the human spirit, which endures longer than dynasties or creeds. The political world of Homer is dead while his song is living to-day. The splendour of Rome has vanished but the poetry of Virgil is yet vital. The dreams of Kālidāsa still move us like the cry of a living voice, with their poignant sense of tears in human relations,

1 Presidential Address at the General Conference in connection with the Seventieth Birthday Celebrations of Rabindranath Tagore, held in Calcutta, December 1931.

while the Ujjain of which he was the ornament has left her memory to his keeping. The great medieval potentates are forgotten, but the song of Dante is still cherished; and the Elizabethan age will be remembered as long as the English language lives on account of its Shakespeare. When our lords and leaders pass into oblivion, Tagore will continue to enchant us by his music and poetry; for though he is an Indian, the value of his work lies not in any tribal or national characteristics, but in those elements of universality which appeal to the whole world. He has added to the sweetness of life, to the stature of civilization.

II

EMPHASIS ON THE SPIRITUAL

To many a young Indian in these changing times Rabindranath's voice has been a comfort and a stimulus. When we are weighed down by the burden of defeated hopes and stand dazed at the conquests of science and organization, when our minds lose their moorings and sense of direction, he comes to us instilling hope into our hearts and courage into our minds. He points out that though our heads are bleeding they are not bowed down, and the value of success need not be judged by standards of wealth and power. The true tests of civilization are spiritual dignity and power of suffering. Wealth, power and efficiency are the appurtenances of life and not life itself. The significant things are the personal ones which are beyond the reach of science and organization.

In his insistence on the supremacy of spiritual values as central to good life and social order, Rabindranath is at one with the long tradition of Indian thinkers. In him we find the eternal voice of India, old and yet new. In spite of the vicissitudes of fortune and the driftings of history, India has kept her essential spirit alive. The self of man is not to be confused with the physical body or the intellect. There is something deeper than intellect, mind and body:—the real self, which is one with the self of all goodness, truth and beauty. To aim at that and make it a living presence is the purpose of religion; to train oneself through purity, love and strength into conformity with that conception is the aim of ethics; to mould oneself to the pattern of that eternal being is the consummation of our aesthetic nature. One has to achieve not merely technical efficiency but greatness of spirit.

When we walk into the night and see the stars keeping their eternal watch, we experience a sense of awe before their remoteness, of annihilation before their immutability, of utter insignificance before their immensity. The heart stops beating, breathing is suspended and our whole being receives a shock. Our petty interests and anxieties look pitifully small and sordid. There is a similar perturbation, a similar break in the breath, when we listen to great poetry or gaze into a human soul. Philosophy and religion, art and literature, serve to heighten this spiritual consciousness. It is because we have ignored this aspect of life that we find to-day so much instability, conflict and chaos in spite of intellectual advance and scientific progress. For over three centuries scientific inventions and discoveries have produced increased prosperity. Famines have practically disappeared, population has increased and the grimmer incidents of life like plagues and pestilences have been brought under control. As the sense of confidence and security about the social order spread over the world, the spirit of curiosity and exploration, which was mainly responsible for the triumphs in the scientific and the technical regions, became extended to the deeper things of life. The world was soon robbed of its mystery and romance. A strange new world of hardness and brutality, of science and big business arose, which prejudiced the order of love, beauty and happiness so very essential for the growth of the soul. Scepticism and agnosticism have become attractive to the modern mind. In the struggle between the sceptics and agnostics who doubt whether there is anything behind the universe, and the spiritual positivists who affirm that the most vital reality is behind the universe, Rabindranath is with the latter.

There is a story about the visit of an Indian Philosopher to Socrates. It comes not from Plato or Xenophon but from Aristoxenes of the third century

B.C. He relates that Socrates told the Indian stranger that his work consisted in enquiring about the life of men, and the Indian smiled and said that none could understand things human who did not understand things divine. For the whole Western tradition, man is essentially a rational being, one who can think logically and act upon utilitarian principles. In the East, spiritual understanding and sympathy are of more importance than intellectual ability. For thousands who talk, one can think; for thousands who think, perhaps one sees and understands. What distinguishes man is this capacity for understanding.

Physical growth and intellectual efficiency cannot satisfy us. Even if we have extensive agriculture and efficient transportation and every one possesses his own aeroplane and radio set, if all disease is eradicated, if workmen receive doles and pensions and every one lives to a green old age, there will still be unsatisfied aspirations, wistful yearnings. Man does not live by bread alone or by learning alone. We may reorganize the world on the most up-to-date and efficient scientific lines, and make of it a vast commercial house where all the multiple activities of the human atoms are arranged for, so that we have in it every group from the scullery-maids and the errand boys doing their work in the basement cellars, up to the women of fashion making up their faces in the beauty parlours on the top floor, and may even succeed in transforming a

133

society of human beings into a swarm of ants; yet there will be unsatisfied longings, a thirst for ultimates. Even in that new world-order, children will continue to laugh and cry, women to love and suffer, men to fight and struggle. The real greatness of man is due to his failure, to his moving about in worlds unrealized, with vague misgivings. Man is a creature with a dual status. He partakes of the characters of both the seen and the unseen worlds. While he is a part of the natural order, he has in him the seed of spirit which makes him dissatisfied with his merely natural being. He is truly "a creature of the borderland," with animal desires and spiritual yearnings; and a life which is entirely given over to the former cannot give him rest.

In his daily life of work and toil, when he tills the soil or governs the State, when he seeks wealth or pursues power, man is not himself. In such activities things are in the saddle. The making of money and the tending of families absorb all the time and strength. Things eternal and unseen get no chance. And yet events occur which disturb the complacency of superficial minds, events with which the sense of mystery and the feeling of uncertainty return. When in the sorrow of death or the suffering of despair, when trust is betrayed or love desecrated, when life becomes tasteless and unmeaning, man stretches forth his hands to heaven to know if perchance there is an answering presence behind the dark clouds; *mahāntam puruṣam ādityavarṇam tamasaḥ parastāt*—it is then that he comes into touch with the supreme in the solitude of his consciousness, in the realm of the profound and the intense. It is the world of light and love in which there is no language but that of silence. It is the world of joy that reveals itself in innumerable forms, *anandarūpaam amṛtam yad vibhāti*.

The poetry of human experience, the realities of life as distinct from its mere frills, are achieved in solitude. When we move away from the self, we move away from the only reality which is accessible to us. Man is himself in his religion and in his love. Both these are strictly personal and intimate, peculiar and sacred. If our society attempts to invade even this inner sanctuary, life will lose all its worth and genuineness. A man can share his possessions with others, but not his soul.

We have become so poor to-day that we cannot even recognize the treasures of spirit. In the rush and clamour of our conscious life we do not pay attention to the less audible elements of our being. The sudden thrills, the disturbing emotions, the flashes of insight, it is these that reveal to us the mystery we are, and by these we apprehend the truth of things.

Only the man of serene mind can realize the spiritual meaning of life. Honesty with oneself is the condition of spiritual integrity. We must let in the light to illumine the secret places of the soul. Our pretensions and professions are the barriers that shut us away from truth. We are more familiar with the things we have than with what we are. We are afraid to be alone with ourselves, face to face with our naked loneliness. We try to hide from ourselves the truth by drugs or drunkenness, excitement or service. It is with an effort that we have to pull ourselves together, cultivate the inner life, and abstract from the outer sheaths of body, mind and intellect. We then see the soul within and attain to a stillness of spirit. The discovery of inwardness is the essential basis of spiritual life.

So long as we lead outward lives, without being touched to our inward depths, we do not understand the meaning of life or the secrets of the soul. Those who live on the surface naturally have no faith in the life of spirit. They believe that they do their duty by religion if they accept the letter of faith. Such spiritual dependence is inconsistent with true religious life, of which the foundation is utter sincerity. A life without independent thought cannot comfort a spiritual being. It is lack of spiritual confidence that impels us to accept what others say about religious truth. But when once the individual in his freedom of spirit pursues truth and builds up a centre in himself, he has enough strength and stability to deal with all that happens to him. He is able to retain his peace and power even when he is faced by adverse conditions. Absolute serenity of spirit is the ultimate goal of human effort, and this is possible only for one who has deep faith in the creative spirit and is thus free from all petty desires. Naturally orthodox religion, whether as dogma or ritual, means almost nothing to him.

III

INSISTENCE ON LIFE

But to dwell in the realm of spirit does not mean that we should be indifferent to the realities of the world. It is a common temptation, to which Indian thinkers have fallen more than once victims, that spirit is all that counts while life is an indifferent illusion, and all efforts directed to the improvement of man's outer life and society are sheer folly. Frequently the ideal of the cold wise man who refuses all activity in the world is exalted, with the result that India has become the scene of a culture of dead men walking the earth which is peopled with ghosts. No one who holds himself aloof from the activities of the world and who is insensitive to its woes can be really wise. To practise virtue in a vacuum is impossible. Spiritual vision normally issues in a new power for good in the world of existence. The spiritual man does not turn his back on the realities of the world, but works in it with the sole object of creating better material and spiritual conditions. For spiritual life rises in the natural. Being a poet, Rabindranath uses the visible world as a means of shadowing forth the invisible. He touches the temporal with the light of the eternal.

The material world becomes transparent as his spirit moves in it.

The world is not a snare nor its good a delusion. They are opportunities for self-development, pathways for realization. This is the great tradition which has come down from the seers of the Upaniṣads and the author of the Gītā. They delight in life. For since God has taken upon Himself the bonds of creation, why should we not take upon ourselves the bonds of this world? We need not complain, if we are clothed in this warm garment of flesh. Human relationships are the mainspring of spiritual life. God is not a Sultan in the sky but is in all, through all and over all. We worship Him in all the true objects of our worship, love Him whenever our love is true. In the woman who is good, we feel Him; in the man who is true we know Him. Tagore's Hibbert Lectures on *The Religion of Man* (1931) ask us to realize the supreme in the heart of us all.

The great of the world work in it sensitive to its woes. When Buddha preaches *maitri* and the Gītā teaches *sneha* for all, they mean that we can understand others only through love. To look upon life as an evil and treat the world as a delusion is sheer ingratitude. In his play *Saññyāsi or the Ascetic*, Rabindranath points out how outraged nature had her revenge on the ascetic who tried to gain a victory over her by cutting away the bonds of human desires and affections. He attempted to arrive at a true knowledge of the world by cutting himself off from

138

it. A little girl brought him back from this region of abstraction into the play of life. No asceticism is ever equal to the task of suppressing living beauty The ascetic's inmost defences went down before the rapture of beauty, and clamant life compelled him to fling open the doors. The Saññyāsi discovered that "the great is to be found in the small, the infinite within the bounds of form and the eternal freedom of the soul in love." We must bring heaven down to earth, put eternity into an hour and realize God in this world. Ascetics are like cut flowers in metal vases. They are beautiful to contemplate for a while but they soon wither, being without nourishment from the soil. To be firm and rooted, man must consent to be nourished of life. Asceticism, however necessary it may be for the growth of the person, cannot be confused with a mere refusal of the nourishment by which the growth is helped. The saints do not refuse to sit at the rich man's table; nor do they object to the scent of precious ointment.

It is foolish to fancy that God enjoys our sorrows and sufferings, our pains and fasts, and loves those who tax themselves to the uttermost. Life is a great gift, and those who do not love it are unworthy of it. Those who lay waste their souls and call it peace cannot obtain the support of Tagore for their action.

One need not enter a convent or become an ascetic to reject life. Many of us reject life by surrounding ourselves with taboos and prohibitions. Interpreting the main intention of Hindu thought, Tagore insists on a loyal acceptance of life. We must face life as an adventure and give full play to its possibilities.

Religion speaks to us in many dialects. It has diverse complexions. And yet it has one true voice, the voice of human pity and compassion, of mercy, of patient love, and to that voice we must do all we can to listen. Naturally, a sensitive soul is bound to be outraged by the social order which is at the end of one age and the beginning of another. We say that there is a revolution in Russia or Spain; but there is one in our country too. We also have our guillotines and our victims, though many of those who suffer still go about with their heads on their shoulders. We have become mere walking and talking phantoms. With our languid paleness and lack of depth, which we try to cover by paint and pose, our lives remind us of the mannequins displayed in the shop windows of Chowringhee.

Our deepest passions are debased by the conditions imposed by society. Add to this the appalling poverty and ignorance in which many people live. If they are somewhat sensitive in temper, they are compelled to spend perturbed nights of anguish and long monotonous days of struggle measuring time by the throbs of pain and the memories of bitterness. When dim thoughts of suicide rush through their overcrowded heads, they stare at the ceiling and smoke a cigarette. Rabindranath has not much sympathy with the prevalent view that social service consists simply in joining leagues to stop cigarette smoking or to advance the practice of birth control. It consists in enabling people to live with intensity of being.

As a poet he despises organization and believes in each man living his own life in his own way. He is the champion of the individual in his age-long struggle against the mass tyranny which crushes him. The fate of one who sets himself against the established order is abuse and criticism, persecution and fierce solitariness. Tagore is the poet of sorrow and suffering. The pathos of men's striving, the bitterness of life submerged in the shadows, the waste and loneliness of women's lives have found few more profoundly moved spectators. To this audience it is scarcely necessary to refer to the innumerable instances where the poet reveals the anguish that is implicit in common situations.

The most sacred of all human relationships is love; and whatever our scriptures may say, our practice is immoral because it demands the beauties of self-control and self-abnegation from only one sex. So long as our women are treated as mere servants and toys of the undisciplined male, the social order will continue to be corrupt. The convention that a woman's virtues are chastity and submissiveness to man is altogether too flimsy an excuse for masculine tyranny. What is virtue in a man is virtue in a woman. It is unfortunate that there are many among us who are cold-blooded libertines who unscrupulously use women as instruments of their lust. They are the human animals, the slaves of sense.

The body is the temple of the spirit, the apparatus for spiritual growth. To regard the body or any part of it as indecent or vile is the sin of impiety. To treat it as cheap and vulgar is equally impious. Physical union without love is the essence of prostitution. This is true within as without marriage. A woman who gives herself to a man for whom she has no love, as a mere act of duty just because she is his wife, is as cruelly abusing herself as the husband who insists on his rights. Love is spiritual and aesthetic, a matter of conscience and good taste and not one of law or codes. Married life without love is like slave labour. Obedience to ecclesiastical pundits or social rules is a form of self-indulgence, even as action in obedience to one's deepest being is the imperative command of life. As beauty is higher than harmony, as truth is higher than consistency, so is love higher than law. Like fire it purifies everything.

In his play *Sati*, Uma refuses to accept the man who never won her love even though he was her chosen husband, whatever pledges others may have given for her. When she cuts herself away from Jivaji to whom she was sacredly affianced and accepts another, she defends herself by saying, "my body was yielded only after love had given me." When her mother says, "Touch me not with impure hands," she replies, "I am as pure as yourself."

Her eloquent and dignified bearing cuts her father to the quick and he says: "Come to me, my darling child! mere vanity are these man-made laws, splashing like spray against the rock of heaven's ordinance." Our legal providers and protectors do not realize that our women possess souls, yearning for understanding, for some one to share their dreams and their longings; and when a man and a woman offer to each other, not their strength or rank or fortune but their weakness, their desolation, their heart's need, they enter into a region which is not built by the labour of human hands but by the love of their hearts. Their union is consecrated though it may not be approved.

IV

CONCLUSION

In all Rabindranath's work three features are striking. (1) The ultimateness of spiritual values to be obtained by inward honesty and cultivation of inner life; (2) the futility of mere negation or renunciation and the need for a holy or a whole development of life; and (3) the positive attitude of sympathy for all, even the lowly and the lost. It is a matter for satisfaction to find an Indian leader insisting on these real values of life at a time when so many old things are crumbling away and a thousand new ones are springing up.

INDEX

GEORGE ALLEN & UNWIN LTD
London: 40 Museum Street, WC1

Auckland: P.O. Box 36013, Northcote Central, N.4
Barbados: P.O. Box 222, Bridgetown
Bombay: 15 Graham Road, Ballard Estate, Bombay 1
Buenos Aires: Escritorio 454-459, Florida 165
Calcutta: 17 Chittaranjan Avenue, Calcutta 13
Cape Town: 68 Shortmarket Street
Hong Kong: 105 Wing On Mansion, 26 Hankow Road, Kowloon
Ibadan: P.O. Box 62
Karachi: Karachi Chambers, McLeod Road
Madras: Mohan Mansions, 38c Mount Road, Madras 6
Mexico: Villalongin 32-10, Piso, Mexico 5, D.F.
Nairobi: P.O. Box 4536
New Delhi: 13-14 Asaf Ali Road, New Delhi 1
Ontario: 81 Curlew Drive, Don Mills
Rio de Janeiro: Caixa Postal, 2537-Zc-00
São Paulo: Caixa Postal 8675
Singapore: 36c Prinsep Street, Singapore 7
Sydney, N.S.W.: Bradbury House, 55 York Street
Tokyo: P.O. Box 26, Kamata

by *Radhakrishnan*

THE HINDU VIEW OF LIFE

Cr 8vo

' It should be studied by missionaries and others who have the high and responsible task of representing our culture in the East . . . An admirable exposition of the basis of Aryan philosophy.' *The Spectator*

' If what he describes in such masterly English and in such a scholarly and lucid way really be Hinduism, then there are many thousands of Friends who belong to that religion, though they call themselves Christians.' *Friend*

AN IDEALIST VIEW OF LIFE

Hibbert Lectures   *Demy 8vo*

' I consider the book to be one of the most original and significant contributions to modern thought. Personally I am deeply grateful to it for the benefit I have derived from the beauty and lucidity as well as the wide range of its philosophical insight.' DR. RABINDRANATH TAGORE

' Beautifully written, comprehensively thought, and of high value.' *The Scotsman*

' Professor Radhakrishnan possesses the rare gift of being able to make righteousness readable, and I know of no work which, while so fairly and crisply presenting the modern criticism of religion, presents also with such an eloquence of passionate conviction the modern reply. The result is one of the most profoundly moving religious books of our time.' C. E. M. JOAD in *The Spectator*

by *Radhakrishnan*

INDIAN PHILOSOPHY IN TWO VOLUMES

Revised Second Edition   *Demy 8vo*

'An excellent book upon which author, editor and publisher are to be heartily congratulated. Professor Radhakrishnan has treated a great subject with admirable clarity and excellent judgment. He has given us an interpretation of Indian thought and aspiration that is vivid, vital, gripping.' *Journal of Philosophy*

'The work is admirably done.' BERTRAND RUSSELL in *The Nation*

'This is the first time that an Indian philosopher, well equipped in European philosophy, has tried to present to the modern world the thoughts of the ancient Indian philosophers in a systematic way.' *Theosophist*

RELIGION AND SOCIETY

Illustrated   *Demy 8vo*

'A highly stimulating and deeply satisfying book. If one wishes to see the great problems that face mankind to-day through the eyes of one steeped in both the wisdom of the East and the philosophy of the West, there is probably no one more competent to give us that insight than Professor Radhakrishnan.' *The Inquirer*

'Professor Radhakrishnan's work is the fruit of deep religious conviction and a fine philosophical intellect equally at home in East and West.' *Manchester Guardian*

Edited by Radhakrishnan

HISTORY OF PHILOSOPHY: EASTERN AND WESTERN

IN TWO VOLUMES   *Sm. Roy. 8vo*

The first step towards the evolution of One World is the establishment of unity in the world of thought. *History of Philosophy: Eastern and Western* therefore aims at a broad review of Man's philosophical quest from the dawn of history. Japan and China, India and Persia, Greece and Arabia, Palestine and Egypt, Europe and America, are all brought together in one comprehensive picture of the philosophy of the world.

The result of the co-operation of some sixty scholars drawn from several countries, this is perhaps the first book in which Indian scholars attempt a systematic interpretation of the teachings of the master minds of the west, side by side with penetrating studies in topics of Indian and other Oriental schools of philosophy.

THE BHAGAVADGĪTĀ

La. Cr. 8vo

In the re-spiritualization of the world, the Bhagavadgītā will have a considerable influence. Professor Radhakrishnan, the greatest living interpreter of Indian thought, who is equally at home in the European and Asiatic traditions of thought, provides an authoritative and inspiring guide to the meaning and message of the Bhagavadgītā. This volume gives us the Sanscrit text, an English translation and an original commentary which may well become a classic on the subject.

THE PRINCIPAL UPANISADS

Edited by Radhakrishnan

Muirhead Library of Philosophy　　　　　　　　*Demy 8vo*

The Upaniṣads are the earliest documents which speak to us of the splendours of the world of spirit, which transcends the differences of tongues. They illustrate the maxim that truth is one though it shines in many forms. Each generation sees in them something a little different from the preceding and our generation, which is in search of a purer and deeper religion, will find in the Upaniṣads the broad outlines of a religion of spirit which will bind peoples together.

' This book will, I believe, remain for many years a standard and authoritative edition of the principal Upaniṣads and an indispensable aid to the Western student of Indian religion; and what greater and more understanding mind could we desire to lead us through these otherwise difficult Indian scriptures than India's greatest religious philosopher, Radhakrishnan? '

Congregational Quarterly

RECOVERY OF FAITH

by Radhakrishnan

World Perspectives　　　　　　　　*Crown 8vo*

In this inspiring book, one of the most brilliant of modern philosophers and statesmen gives an answer to man's need for a new faith.

He exposes the pretensions of communism and explores the inner meanings of Hinduism, Judaism, Christianity, Taoism and other beliefs. He shows how, out of these enduring spiritual expressions, a religion can be achieved which will satisfy humanity's aspirations by transcending dogmatic and sectarian differences.

CONTEMPORARY INDIAN
PHILOSOPHY

Edited by Radhakrishnan and J. H. Muirhead

Library of Philosophy   *Demy 8vo*

' A book edited by two such thinkers testifies its own
worth. It deals with art and psychology, as well as
philosophy . . . The whole thing is a glowing testimony
to the freshness and vitality of Indian thought in the
twentieth century.' *London Mercury*

' An important challenge to educated India while being
a contribution to philosophical investigation.' *Time and
Tide*

Apart from its technical value in the field of philosophy,
the publication has a certain political importance, as
India stands to-day both in politics and in philosophy at
the opening of a new era in her history. The book, it is
hoped, will contribute to a better mutual understanding
between the whole mind of East and West.

RADHAKRISHNAN : An Anthology
by A. N. Marlow

Cr. 8vo

This volume of studies in comparative philosophy is
presented in honour of this great thinker whose whole
life has been devoted to the cause of philosophy and
international understanding. It is fitting that they should
be concerned with a new line of philosophical activity
which, it is hoped, will ultimately result in a systematic
and harmonious synthesis of East and West.

The contributors include : E. A. Burtt, Charles A. Moore,
K. J. Spalding, M. Hiriyanna, A. C. Mukerji, H. H.
Dubs, Humayan Kabir and P. T. Raju.

GEORGE ALLEN AND UNWIN LTD